THE
SPIRITUAL
FRONTIER

By *Allen Spraggett with William V. Rauscher*
Arthur Ford: The Man Who Talked with the Dead

By *Allen Spraggett*
The Case for Immortality
The World of The Unexplained
Kathryn Kuhlman: The Woman Who Believes in Miracles
Probing The Unexplained
The Bishop Pike Story
The Unexplained

THE SPIRITUAL FRONTIER

William V. Rauscher

WITH

Allen Spraggett

DOUBLEDAY & COMPANY, INC.

GARDEN CITY, NEW YORK

1975

Library of Congress Cataloging in Publication Data
Rauscher, William V
    The spiritual frontier.
    Bibliography: p. 186
      1.   Psychical research.   2.   Occult sciences.
I. Spraggett, Allen, joint author.   II.   Title.
BF1031.R27   133
ISBN 0-385-07189-2
Library of Congress Catalog Card Number 73–15361

To my parents, William and Marie,
and to *Resolute Amender* . . .
who knows why

Acknowledgments

There are many who had a part, large or small, in the creation of this book. To mention all or even most of them would be impossible. However to some I must say thank you:

William Akins and Martin Ebon: for encouragement.

Ruth Hagy Brod, and my agent, Anita Diamant: for opening doors.

Alex Liepa: for editorial guidance.

The Reverend Canon Robert J. Lewis, who has helped me make sense of all this.

Verna Schmidt: who holds the world's typewriting mileage record for church secretaries.

The Reverend John E. Bird, my curate: who has been patient with my psychic pursuits.

My parishioners: many of whom will be surprised by this book but some of whom won't be. . . .

And last but not least, thanks to Allen Spraggett, for many things.

CONTENTS

THE
SPIRITUAL
FRONTIER

1

PROLOGUE
A Door Opens

There was something sinister about that night even before things started to happen.

Maybe it was just a mood evoked by the atmosphere: the full moon, the murmur of the ocean breaking on the New Jersey shore, and the monotonous voice of the hypnotist weaving its spell.

Or maybe it was something else that sent a premonitory shiver through me.

There was no evident reason for me to be uneasy, to anticipate problems in this particular experiment in ESP and hypnosis that hadn't arisen in previous ones I had observed.

The medical hypnotist, whom I knew well, was certainly competent in his skill; and the subject, his wife, had served as a willing guinea pig in many similar experiments. Why, then, the worry?

I didn't know. But as the hypnotist proceeded to put his subject into the familiar sleeplike state, I felt something unwelcome in the room . . . an unfriendly presence.

The subject was no sooner in a deep hypnotic trance than she suffered a bizarre seizure. Her arms and legs twitched, her body convulsed, and her eyes popped open to reveal only the whites. From her lips came a horrible rasping wheeze like escaping air, as though the breath were being squeezed out of her by an invisible python.

Was it a hysterical fit of some kind? Hypnotic melodrama, perhaps, in which subjects have been known to indulge?

No, I wanted to believe that, but what was happening to the woman before our eyes was more than hysteria and certainly no act. It was too real, too unspeakably macabre.

As we watched, that hypnotized subject became someone else. And then, peering out at us from wild, burning eyes was a stranger.

The stranger spoke.

"I am in this body now."

My nerves jumped. The voice, though it came from the woman's lips, was not hers. This voice was hollow, unearthly. Dead.

"I am in this brain," it said.

The woman's hands pawed her head, then patted it, intimately, almost obscenely.

"I am in these hands."

Now, in some sinister thrall, the woman was staring at her hands as though for the first time, turning them over, examining them, it seemed, line by line and vein by vein.

The hypnotist, who obviously had never experienced anything like this before, roused himself from a state of temporary shock to try to restore his control over the subject. He followed the prescribed textbook procedure for handling an unruly subject: remain calm and speak firmly, knowing that the subject must obey the suggestions given.

But this subject refused to obey.

Ignoring the hypnotist's command to awaken from the

trance, still staring at her hands, she crooned in that sepulchral voice:

"I am in these hands . . . in these hands . . . in these hands."

The scene was from a nightmare. But I couldn't escape by pinching myself.

Now the hypnotist, plainly desperate, his voice frayed with emotion, almost shouted his commands.

"Leave the woman! Whoever you are, go! At once!"

Suddenly, her eyes shooting icy sparks, the subject whirled on the hypnotist and hissed:

"I am in this body."

The words dripped defiance, malevolence.

His façade of confidence crumbling, the hypnotist turned to me and pleaded: "Do something! For God's sake, help my wife!"

Suddenly a howl ripped through the room.

"*I cannot find the light!*"

It was the wail of someone unimaginably wounded. The hypnotized woman, her face a mask of agony, clawed the air.

"I am in these eyes but I cannot find the light, I'm shut out from the light," she moaned. "Help me to find the light."

With a silent prayer, chillingly conscious of contending with forces not of this world, I stepped forward to help.

"You need have no fear whoever you are," I said, firmly, calmly.

"I am a follower of Christ, our Friend, and it is He Who is the light you seek. Try to find that light."

Then, uttering a short prayer, I committed the vagrant soul not to outer darkness but to the light of Christ.

"Now," I declared in a tone of authority, "you do see the light. Follow the pathway that leads to that light."

The hypnotized woman's eyes, glittering and abnormally large, were darting to and fro.

"You are going toward the light," I persisted. "It is beautiful; it welcomes you."

Now her writhings stopped, her eyes stared into space, fixated.

"You are being received *into* the light," I said, "the perfect light of Christ, which lighteth every man. Depart now in peace."

Time froze; nothing in the room moved; all that could be heard was the soft sound of the sea. Then the woman shuddered and heaved a deep sigh.

The next moment her body crumpled like an empty sack. In the same instant an unseen presence left the room.

Now the hypnotist regained control of his subject easily, and quickly restored her to the waking state. Happily, she had no recall of the dark interlude.

What really happened that night?

An Intrusion from the Shadow Side of Reality?

Well, I believe (and the physician-hypnotist shared this conviction) that we experienced an intrusion from the shadow side of reality. A door normally shut, but left ajar, had admitted an uninvited visitor.

Make no mistake: The psychic world, like the moon, does have its dark side. This is why there is danger for curiosity-seekers—teen-agers looking for kicks, say, who dabble in the occult. The imprudent use of such psychic fads as ouija boards and automatic writing can cause at the least psychological harm, and possibly much more.

As a priest, my exploration of the psychic world has been an essentially spiritual quest, part of an ongoing search for the meaning of life and death, and what comes after. In my investigations I have found much to strengthen faith, as well as some things of which faith should beware.

My psychic research has led me into some, shall we say, exotic paths.

I've hunted ghosts, but, alas, found none who would meet me face to face, indicating, perhaps, that they are more afraid of me than I am of them.

I've had more luck sitting in dark rooms while some of the world's great mediums went into trance and tried to comunicate with the other side; communications have come—some of them irresistible evidence of contact with a dimension beyond death.

I've watched while apparent psychic energy bent a steel spike, ostensibly moved objects without physical aid, and even allegedly conjured up the visible, tangible forms of the dead.

I've thrilled as healing miracles happened before my eyes—congenital deformities corrected, shattered bones restored, cataracts melted from eyes, cancers shriveled.

I've rubbed elbows and brains with some of the most fascinating people you could meet outside the pages of science fiction: the psychic photographer who takes pictures of thoughts . . . the housewife who receives music from such long-dead composers as Liszt and Beethoven . . . seers who tell the future as easily, it seems, as most of us do the past.

In the psychic world I have ranged the spectrum of human experience: fact and fraud . . . evidence and delusion . . . transfiguring goodness and grotesque corruption . . . the most perfect sanity and the uttermost madness. The psychic world embraces the heights and depths and everything in between.

There are, in the church and out, some who wonder about the propriety of a man of God treading such strange paths. But the moon is no less a strange place to man, and can it be less admirable to explore the canyons of man's psyche than to map the mountains of the moon? Can it possibly be right to probe outer space but wrong to explore inner space?

For too long, churchmen have been content to let the psychic world remain "the undiscovered country," the far side of the moon. What do we say now, however, when, with the current popularity of the occult in all its forms, our people come to us for honest, informed guidance?

This personal narrative was written not as a theological tome nor, God forbid, as merely another addition to occult literature, but for one reason: to provide responsible guidance in psychic matters; to map for the spiritual seeker the lights and shadows of the occult world.

Is psychic exploration worthwhile?

Escaping the Prison of the Human Body

On the basis of my own experience, the answer is: It is immeasurably worthwhile. Faith, for me, has been deepened and broadened by my psychic discoveries. What these discoveries have added supremely to my faith has been the vital dimension of personal experience.

It is one thing to believe in human immortality, for example, but quite another to experience it. Consider a psychic experience that took me beyond faith—and death.

One evening, while I was still attending seminary, I returned to my room from visiting a college science instructor of mine who was in the hospital dying.

As I prepared for bed, my thoughts were of this brilliant and wise man to whom I owed a great intellectual debt. It was he who perhaps first showed me why life after death was perfectly credible on grounds of reason as well as of faith. Now he lay dying, and I couldn't help wondering whether soon he would know that he was right. . . .

With such heavy thoughts it was hard to sleep, but finally I dozed off.

Suddenly I was looking down at myself.

Crazy? Yes, but true. I was looking at myself on the bed, below. I was watching myself sleep, my chest rhythmically rising and falling. It was uncanny, but not frightening.

Indeed, I felt exhilarated, in ecstasy. Along with my body, I had shrugged off gravity. Now I was light as a bubble. By using my will, I discovered it was possible for me to move around.

In those first moments of fierce joy I was not conscious of having a body at all—not even one down below, waiting for me. Yet I felt undiminished. There was no sense that part of me was missing. This, I knew, was all of me that really mattered, somehow outside my body. *Me*.

Suddenly I saw my body as a mere container, wonderful in its way, yet still a prison into which I had been squeezed all my life. Now, for the first time, I had room to stretch.

Physical barriers were meaningless. I passed through the walls of the room as easily as a thought would and was outside in the clear winter's night, feeling no cold, for I was beyond cold and heat, rejoicing in my buoyant freedom.

The stars were more quiveringly beautiful than I had ever seen them, or was I seeing them with different eyes? But I knew, as never before, that I was more immortal than the stars.

There was, I understood, an ineffable, perfect plan that contained all that was, is, and is to be, and I was part of it.

This for me, at that moment, was not an act of faith but of *knowing*.

I thought of the seminary chapel, two blocks from my room, where I often prayed and instantly was there, looking down on it, relishing the sight of it and all that it meant to me.

Then, like the guilty thought of an errand undone, something pulled at me. I felt a tug, as though I were a balloon on the end of a string.

I knew I must return. Immediately.

Like an elastic band, that quickly, I snapped back into time and space and was sitting up in bed, wide awake, pondering my marvelous experience.

Had it been a dream?

Never for a moment could I believe that. No, the experience was too lucid, too utterly real. There was nothing in the least dreamlike about it. As a matter of fact, by comparison, my normal waking state seemed the dream.

For those few moments I had been not asleep but, probably for the first time in my life, truly awake.

Parapsychologists call what happened to me an out-of-the-body experience. It has happened to countless other people—psychiatrists (the great Dr. Carl Jung), writers (Ernest Hemingway, Somerset Maugham), scientists (Sir Aukland Geddes), as well as farmers, and bakers, and candlestick makers.

Some have been hurled out of their bodies by the shock of an accident. Some have died and been medically revived. Others have doffed their physical selves during sleep, as I did, or under the influence of drugs, and others have mastered the art of shedding their bodies at will.

The experience leaves everyone who has it, with a profound, know-so conviction: Human personality transcends the limits of the body and, therefore, survives bodily death.

This was for me a luminous spiritual discovery revealed through a psychic experience. There were other discoveries, equally exciting and significant to me, that I want to share with you.

Let me tell you about them in the following chapters.
. . .

2

THE BEGINNING
OF A QUEST

There used to be a radio program called "I Love a Mystery," and as a child I never missed it. And I mean *never*.

The very word "mystery" made me goose-pimply all over.

Boys are supposed to love dogs, swimming, fishing, eating green apples, wrestling, and, in rare cases, getting all A's in school. Well, I was rarer still. I hankered after strange things, odd things, the things that didn't fit in, that were off the beaten track. From as early as I can remember I had this yen for the unfamiliar, the unknown.

This is what led me, I'm sure, into both magic and mysticism. Pulling rabbits out of a hat (which I started before kindergarten and kept up long enough to help pay my way through college and seminary) isn't so far from celebrating holy communion as one might think. Both are based on a mystery, the one trivial and easily solved, the other profound and as inscrutable as life itself.

There is a theory I favor about magicians as a breed: They have a Jehovah complex. They want to be able to perform real magic, and they secretly resent the fact that they can't. You know, dematerialize that elephant without needing ten tons of equipment to do it, or cut that pretty girl in half and restore her as easily as it looks. Inside every magician is a nine-year-old who has never gotten over his luciferian ambition to be God.

The mystic wants to be God, too, of course, but in a profoundly different sense, and herein lies the distinction between the psychology of magic and that of mysticism. The magician wants to be that nine-year-old endowed with godlike powers; the mystic knows that to use such powers properly one should first be godlike.

If I ask myself where and when my love affair with mystery started, I think it came with me at birth. And that, I guess, is another mystery.

There were early incidents that sharpened my appetite for the unknown and the unusual.

In Highlands, New Jersey, where I was raised, my grandfather had a grocery store, and I used to hide from the adult world in its back storeroom—a wonderful place of forgotten things. Once, at the age of ten, I found there on a high shelf a book *How to Hypnotize*.

It occurred to me then that my grandfather must know something other people didn't. But my father warned me not to mention my discovery, for it would make my grandmother angry. Hypnotism was a sore point between my grandparents, apparently.

Once, I gathered, my grandmother had come downstairs in the middle of the night and found my grandfather in the back room, with a group watching, stretching a hypnotized subject rigidly between two chairs. All hell broke loose over that. But later grandfather put a man to sleep for a day in the drugstore window.

When I asked my grandfather to show me what hypnotism was, he said: "It's very simple, Billy; just suggestion."

At that moment a woman came into the store and wanted American cheese. She left with spiced ham, which was more expensive.

"That, Billy," said my grandfather with a pat on the head, "is hypnosis."

It was one of my earliest lessons in the power of the spoken word.

Even before this, I had discovered the delights of magic and annoyed everybody with coin and card tricks. On trips to Newark with my grandfather I haunted a local magic shop. Soon my grandfather took me to the place where the professional wonder-workers bought their equipment, a fourteenth-floor office in New York crammed with all the colored boxes, silks, and gadgets any magic-struck boy could have dreamed of.

The Curious Mystery of the Ministry

Exactly when my love of magic melted into a love of mysticism is hard to say—it was like growing from childhood to young manhood. Since they sprang from the same root, both were probably always there.

At five or six years of age I would pretend to be a priest and, using an orange crate covered with a cloth and draping a towel around my shoulders, I'd pray before the altar.

Too, I remember the curious mystery of the lost crosses. On solitary walks along the ocean shore I would find often—more often than one would expect—a cross someone had lost. I always felt I was meant to find the cross, that no cross should stay lost but should have somebody to care for it. It perplexed my parents that I kept finding these crosses and bringing them home.

My very first experience with the "psychic"—a brush, really—was as a high school student when I visited a fascinating blond lady with a large-brimmed pink hat who had a booth on the boardwalk in Asbury Park, New Jersey. Over the booth hung a sign with the words, in tarnished silver sparkle dust stuck to glue: "*Handwriting Analysis.*"

The mysterious lady, whom I used to see riding up on a bicycle, would scan a sample of one's handwriting and then offer a character analysis.

"Write your name, kid," she said lightly when I plunked my fifty cents down on the counter. Then, chewing on a wad of gum, she looked at my signature, and at me, and said: "Did you ever think of the ministry? If not, you really should, young man, you really should."

The last time I visited the lady whose analysis proved so aptly prophetic two nuns stood, as though debating whether to approach the booth, then did.

The last I heard, the blond lady in the big pink hat was dead. I wonder if she's still analyzing somebody's handwriting, somewhere. . . .

When time for college came, in 1950, and I enrolled at Glassboro State (at which President Johnson and Soviet Premier Alexei Kosygin later were to confer an unaccustomed glamor by holding a summit conference), I hadn't yet made up my mind to enter the priesthood.

Despite the strong tug toward the church, there was a genuine hesitation. One reason, I suppose, was the vague feeling that being a priest would take the fun out of life. And in spite of a Capricornish, sometimes deceptively serious exterior, I do like to have fun.

One professor, who influenced me greatly, and who unwittingly (or maybe not so unwittingly) helped to give me a push toward the priesthood, was George W. Haupt, a member of the college science department. Occasionally I used to do magic shows in the college assembly, and one day he waited for me outside and said: "You know, Rauscher, there is a higher magic." And with that cryptic remark, he stalked off.

Later I discovered that he had a profound knowledge of occultism, mysticism, and psychic research. Though he wasn't big on the organized church, our mutual interests were a special bond, and my association with George Haupt provided another nudge toward the priesthood.

Psychic or Spiritual?

This book is about my psychic explorations, and it was a psychic experience that crystallized my motivation to become a priest. Or it was a spiritual experience, if you prefer. Distinguishing between the two—psychic and spiritual—sometimes isn't easy. If a saint hears angelic voices, it's a spiritual experience; if a psychiatric patient hears voices, angelic or otherwise, it's probably schizophrenia. One experience bears spiritual fruit, while the other is a symptom of spiritual disintegration. The fruit is the test.

Anyway, psychic or spiritual or both (as I believe it was), the experience occurred on a night in December 1952, during my junior year in college. Lying in my room in the "shacks," as we called them (the temporary postwar student residences), I was troubled by the deepest thoughts a young man can think. What shall I do with my life? Is the church for me? Do I love God? Am I qualified for the priesthood? Does God want me there?

Suddenly I was overwhelmed by a sense of being energized. That's what I felt—as though I had touched a high-tension line and currents of electricity were pouring through my body, miraculously not killing but vivifying me. Then there was a physical sensation of light, dazzling, and I was engulfed by it. At that moment my tired body could have lifted the world on its shoulders.

And in the same moment, along with the tremendous sense of being energized and wrapped in light, I knew, suddenly and totally, that the ministry was my path. It was beyond logic, words, or argument. Simply, I knew.

This experience buoyed me up during my trying times in the seminary, especially early in my theological training, when I met only what seemed to me indifference to things which, in my mind, were vital to the church and Christian experience—mystical states, efficacious prayer, sacramental healing, and the survival of human personality after death. Toward these subjects most of my classmates and professors exhibited a profound yawn.

During an acute attack of self-righteousness, one of the afflictions of the young (though not of them only), I went so far as to pack my bags and leave the seminary.

However, two days after I left, I knew I had to go back. The same profound, intense feelings that had swept through me that night when I decided to become a priest now flooded back, stronger than ever. Humbly, with what embarrassment you may imagine, I returned to the seminary and, generously, was readmitted.

On the matter of my psychic and mystic interests, I stood unrepentant, my views unrevised; but now I was in a different frame of mind about the matter. My business was not to proselytize for a point of view, however admirable I deemed it to be, but to follow my own light, while allowing others the same privilege.

Following my own light, I vowed to pursue psychic research in earnest, no matter down how many blind alleys it might lead me. Truth I was prepared to seek from any source that appeared to offer it, whether or not the source was ecclesiastically accredited. In time, this source proved to include Spiritualist mediums, Theosophical lecturers, Hindu yogis, and even Protestant fundamentalists.

"The Necromancer"

My devotion to the historic Catholic faith was undiminished. An Episcopalian, a member of the Anglican communion, I was one to the core, and so remain. But I had come to recognize that the Holy Spirit turns up all over the place, sometimes under the most unlikely auspices, and that the Lord isn't as choosy about His instruments as we are.

When news of my psychic research got out (and seminaries and seminarians being what they are, it did get out), I took some friendly and not-so-friendly ribbing. One classmate gave me a book on a psychic theme with the comment: "This interests me so little you should be wild about it." I was.

An elderly professor, Father Pottle, crotchety but cerebral, dubbed me "that necromancer." I took a perverse pride in the title, suspecting that it was bestowed more in affection than derision and even with a certain respect for a student who at least had convictions of his own.

Inevitably I found, as loners always do, someone else as mad about the psychic as I was. Well, almost. Actually Bob Lewis, a seminarian who had been a philosophy major in college, was immersed more in the influence of the mystics on the Church's life and literature, an interest to which he felt psychic research was vitally relevant. We struck up a deep friendship and intellectual kinship that has continued to this day. (The Reverend Canon Robert Lewis is now rector of his own large parish and a recognized authority on the Church's mystical tradition.)

Lewis and I went on a sort of psychic binge. We attended faith-healing rituals ranging from the intimidatingly intellectual sermons of Christian Science to the frenzied emotionalism of revival meetings. We ran the theological gamut from ever-so-clever left-wing Unitarianism to the esotericism of the United Lodge of Theosophy. From these, and many sources in between, we gleaned truth and were grateful for it.

Then came a milepost in my psychic quest. I met the man who, more than any other, opened up for me the incredible possibilities of psychic experience; the most celebrated and justly acclaimed medium of our time: Arthur Ford.

It was September 1954, and an astrologer, Gertrude R. Meetze, who had just cast my horoscope (and had predicted, by the way, that I would achieve a certain fame for my psychic investigations), urged me to hear Ford when he spoke at a small Spiritualist church in New Jersey. I went, I heard—and I was impressed.

The Spiritualist service was typically, almost embarrassingly, low-brow, but when Ford stepped forward to speak, he gave off sparks. The man was a brilliant lecturer, and his account of some of his mediumistic experiences electrified the audience.

I spoke to him afterward, I confess with some timidity, introducing myself as a student at the Philadelphia Divinity School. Ford fixed me with a penetrating glance and said: "How would you like to come to a private-group sitting I'm giving for some friends? I'll be in trance and then you'll see some real stuff."

I accepted with almost unseemly haste. Accordingly, a week later, Bob Lewis and I turned up at the apartment of one of Ford's friends, Melvin Sutley, administrator of the Wills Eye Hospital in Philadelphia and a long-time student of psychic research.

The Amazing Arthur Ford

There were seventeen people present at that, our first Ford séance, none of whom we knew except the medium himself. For two seminarians, it was a dizzying experience to be thrust suddenly into the vortex of a psychic whirlpool.

Putting a blindfold on, Ford breathed deeply and loudly for a few minutes and appeared to pass into a trance. In this altered state of consciousness, he earlier had told us, he became the mouthpiece for a former friend of his, now dead, called only Fletcher.

When a voice, very much like Ford's but with a trace

of an unplaceable accent, greeted us, one of the experienced sitters responded: "Welcome, Fletcher." Then, without delay, the mysterious Fletcher began giving those in the room messages purporting to come from deceased loved ones and friends.

When he came to Bob Lewis and me, Fletcher-Ford said (I made notes at the time): "There is someone over here who is named after his father. William? Your father's name is William."

That was so, I acknowledged.

"There is a John here," said Fletcher, "an uncle. He's very interested in you and proud that you're here. He sends his love to your mother."

All this, though unspectacular, was quite true. My Uncle John, who was dead, always had been specially fond of my mother and of me.

Fletcher continued: "There is a clergyman very close to you. Did he ever preach in Washington or before Presidents? Christopher Snyder."

Memories from childhood tumbled into my mind. Father Snyder had been the parish priest in Highlands when I was a boy. He and his wife had virtually adopted me, taking me on trips with them, and generally doting on me. It was, humanly speaking, through his influence, largely, that I was in the seminary.

The reference to preaching before Presidents was striking. I recognized it as an allusion to the Church of the Presidents in Elberon, New Jersey, of which Father Snyder for a time was parish priest. The church was so named because of the many Chief Executives who had worshiped there over the years.

Now, communicating directly through Arthur Ford, the entranced medium, Father Snyder said: "I am having a good time with Randall. Randall Conklin. Do you know his son Randy yet?"

Father Snyder, I recalled, had studied with a priest named Randall Conklin, once rector of Trinity Parish,

Asbury Park, New Jersey. At the time I didn't know his
son. But curiously—and this is the sort of odd coincidence,
if that's what is was, associated with Arthur Ford's mediumship—I made his acquaintance when my first church
neighbored his.

The communicator spoke at length about his feelings
when he realized he was dead.

> It is remarkable how quickly one can adjust to
> the idea that life goes on. I had a great feeling of
> relief. The new life isn't so different from the
> old! It's a projection of the best that you are
> into a new dimension. We are moving on over
> here, growing. Remember that always. . . .
>
> Every day is judgment day. That's the lesson
> we see clearly here. Your judgment day is the
> day you choose, the day you make any moral
> decision. That's absolute justice.

There was a prophecy for Bob Lewis: "You'll make a
great contribution to the ministry. With your love of
music, you will make a contribution to the liturgy and
ritual. The Gospel is the most beautiful thing in the
world, and it should be presented the most beautifully."

The communication ended with another word to me:
"Bishop Gardner is a fine man. He didn't accept things
here so quickly, but he'll come around. Just like the old
codger!"

"Daniel McGregor is here. He kept the seminary up.
He had an educational program."

Some of these remarks were evidential to me. Gardner
was the name of Father Snyder's bishop, who recently
had died. The bishop and the rector had numerous quar-
rels about the preservation of the Church of the Presidents, and Father Snyder often referred to him as an "old
codger," though in reality his love for Bishop Gardner was
warm and deep.

Who Was Daniel McGregor?

The reference to Daniel McGregor meant nothing to me at the time, though, as I'll describe, it soon did.

Fletcher's prediction that Bob Lewis would make a contribution to the liturgy materalized in a very short time when he was asked to be cantor for the seminary services and later became curate in a very ceremonial parish.

However, back to the puzzler: the item about Daniel McGregor. Who was he? Lewis and I decided to ask the one whose knowledge of the seminary's history surpassed any other's: Father Pottle, he who had bestowed on me the title of necromancer.

Eccentric, something like a character out of Dickens, but kindly, and formidably intellectual, Pottle lived in a small apartment that was always overflowing with books. His two vices, eminently forgivable, were the pipe and German beer, both of which he indulged with relish. Mixed with the scholarly tomes on his bookshelves, I noticed, were plenty of ghost stories, and when he told us that he never went to bed without a crucifix, I wondered if he really were afraid of evil spirits.

Anyway, Father Pottle had no difficulty remembering the man in whom we were interested. Many years ago, he said, this McGregor had accepted a call to teach at the seminary and arrived bag and baggage only to be told that the board of trustees had hired someone else. McGregor left and went to work for another educational department of the Church.

With this bit of data, we scored Arthur Ford's accuracy at virtually 100 per cent. Was it due to chance? An unusual streak of lucky guessing on his part? ESP? Or communication from the dead?

It wasn't until many séances later that I concluded that Arthur Ford, at least sometimes, truly did communicate with discarnate spirits. My reasons for so believing are presented in the chapter on mediumship, "Do the Dead Communicate?"

It seems that when around psychic people one tends personally to become more psychic, as though it were contagious, like measles.

It was after Bob Lewis and I had rubbed shoulders with Arthur Ford that there occurred an extraordinary spontaneous psychic phenomenon that strengthened our belief in both the reality of such experiences and their value as evidence of human survival after death.

The experience is so remarkable—so uncanny, even— that I ask you to consider it with a totally open mind.

Bob Lewis's Grandmother

When the time came for our canonical examinations, which would determine whether or not we were to proceed to ordination, Bob Lewis and I took them in our respective dioceses. Fortunately, the exams, conducted by the bishop and his examining chaplains, contained no question about psychic interests (which in those days might have been considered fatally compromising), and the verdict was favorable: I would be ordained.

Happy, and wanting to compare exam questions with Lewis, I went to his room in another seminary building, St. Paul's House, and, finding him not yet returned, sat down in an easy chair to wait.

Dozing, I was awakened by Bob entering the room. We compared notes on the exams—he had passed his, too—and then he told me that all day his grandmother had been in his thoughts.

Bob's grandmother, a devout, Welsh-born Baptist from Taylor, Pennsylvania, raised him and was the central figure in his childhood. She was an emotional woman who, when she felt very happy, wept. Whenever Bob did something that made her specially proud: tears. Bob recalled that when he told her he was going to enter the ministry, she shed more tears than he had ever seen.

His grandmother had been dead for over a year now, and Bob, fresh from the exams that made his ordination certain, told me that he couldn't help thinking how happy and proud of him she would have been at that moment. He wished she were there to share his happiness.

Then he got up and walked over to the dresser, taking off his tie. He glanced at the photograph of his grandmother that was always on top of the dresser. From my chair, I couldn't see any change in the picture, but suddenly Bob whirled and demanded: "Who's playing a joke? Who's been fooling around with my grandmother's picture?"

Nonplused, I assured him nobody had been in the room since my arrival, and I went over to see what was troubling him. I was astounded! The photograph of Bob's grandmother was soaking wet, dripping, with a small pool of water spreading on the dresser under it.

Examining the picture, we found that it was wet *inside* the glass. That was genuinely puzzling. The back of the picture, made of a dyed imitation velvet, was so wet the velvet had streaked and faded.

Removed from its frame, the photograph didn't dry quickly. When it did dry, the area about the face remained puffed, as though the water had originated there and run downward—from the eyes.

Incredible? A defiance of the known laws of physics?

Perhaps. But it happened. And that night, Bob Lewis's prayers took on a deeper meaning. His grandmother, he knew, was aware of his forthcoming ordination and was happy.

So happy, she had cried.

3

THE QUEST CONTINUES
My Psychic Parishioners

When the late Bishop James Pike crashed into the headlines with the claim that he had communicated with his dead son (through Arthur Ford, a story told in a later chapter), he was accused of thirsting after signs and wonders.

Nothing, retorted the notoriously skeptical bishop, could have been farther from the truth.

"I didn't go seeking anything," Pike told me. "When my son died, I believed he was dead beyond recall. At the time, you see, I reluctantly had given up belief in life after death because I just couldn't see any evidence for it. The last thing in the world I expected was anything odd or 'psychic' to happen to me."

But it did happen. Unbidden, and at first, not understood, mysterious poltergeist phenomena broke out in the apartment in Cambridge, England, that the bishop for several months had shared with his son.

Clocks stopped at the time of the son's death. Postcards written by him mysteriously turned up where they had no business being. Milk unaccountably soured. Bishop Pike and two witnesses saw the dead boy's shaving mirror move from the top of a dresser, apparently of its own accord, and "slither" down the side of the dresser gently to the floor.

It was only after these experiences—which for Pike were not only unsought and unexpected but distinctly unwelcome, since they made him briefly doubt his sanity—that America's most famous ecclesiastical "heretic" turned to a medium for help.

Can It Happen to Anyone?

The point is that psychic experiences, like the wind, blow where they will. They happen to people who may not in the least want them to happen, nor even believe that they can happen.

(An ironic case in point is that of the priest who after hearing me speak on ESP sent me a "Get Well" card. Six years later, told that this same priest was being terrorized by unexplained footsteps in his church, I mailed his "Get Well" card back to him!)

Many people apparently are open to psychic experiences on the unconscious level, even when they shut and bolt the door against them on the conscious level. Or perhaps when a powerful psychic experience comes along, it simply kicks open the door. At any rate, I learned early in my parish ministry that psychic experiences, like the common cold, were bound to turn up.

So many turned up, in fact, among my early parishioners, that the reports reaching me sounded like an introduction to a textbook on parapsychology. Apparitions, messages from the dead, healings, visions, prophetic dreams—all happened.

During this period I was, in a way, serving my internship as a pastoral psychic counselor, and that first parish was a clinic.

The parish was in Florence, New Jersey, a mill town to which the bishop sent me after ordination with instructions to try to bring the dead back to life. There I soon discovered that among Episcopalians (and some others, I suspect), the eighth deadly sin is sleeping late on Sunday mornings.

Those who did appear in church were the proverbial faithful few. And it was among and through these people that I shared some of the most memorable spiritual encounters of my life—experiences that more often than not had heavy psychic overtones.

I discovered, significantly, that many parishioners who have an unusual spiritual or psychic experience may avoid discussing it with their priest for fear he won't understand, will be incredulous, or even will be critical.

Soon after I came to the parish, one of my acolytes (or altar boys) confided that as a small lad he had seen Jesus and never forgotten the experience. Asking his parents about the story, I found some reluctance on their part to discuss it. One aunt, they confided, a hyperreligious type, curiously, was so frightened by the boy's experience that she hadn't entered their home since.

It was my opportunity to reassure these good people, who for years had been secretly troubled by the overreaction of a hysterical relative, that their son was not "odd." Even if we called his vision a dream or hallucination, I explained, it was nonetheless real. And, more important, from talking to the boy it was evident to me that the experience had been a symptom not of some sinister abnormality but of a deep, sincere spirituality. In my judgment, I said, the boy's vision of Christ had helped him to lead a healthier, more rewarding religious life.

Question No. 1, then, for anybody concerned about whether a particular "psychic" experience is good or bad:

Does it help or hinder the individual in living a happier, more fulfilling life? When weighing the spiritual value of psychic happenings, the criterion should be: "By their fruits ye shall know them."

This test served to reassure our church cleaning lady, whom I met one morning in the sanctuary when she was in a state of near-hysteria. Yet, obviously distraught though she was, she had about her an unmistakable radiance, as though her skin were translucent and through it a light was shining.

Hardly able to talk, her words stumbling over themselves, she told me that a moment before, while scrubbing the floor, she looked up and plainly saw Jesus standing there, watching her, and smiling. The sight of Him, she said, took her breath away. The experience had left her shaken—but glowing.

On the basis of her immediate reaction, and, more important, the long-term good influence that the experience proved to have on her spiritual and psychological health, I told her to accept her vision gratefully, with an untroubled mind.

A Spiritual Communion

Even priests, though often a good deal more skeptical about visions and voices than their parishioners, have unusual spiritual experiences—more often, one suspects and hopes, than is generally known. Though, as must be plain by now, I am less skeptical than some priests, I still treat unusual spiritual experiences with respectful caution, initially at least. But I have had my share. Or more.

Once, for example, I went to the home of an ill parishioner to administer the sacrament of holy communion to her. As I performed the service, a most peculiar feeling crept over me. It was not in the least a negative sensation, simply very strange.

I "felt," and at the same time seemed to see, what can only be described as a ray of light streaming from a nearby photograph of the communicant's dead husband into my hand, into the communion wafer, and thence into her. It were as though, in the act of holy communion, that that was indeed what was taking place—a spiritual communion, real, powerful, between the woman and her deceased husband. The "ray" may have been a hallucinatory image formed by my unconscious mind, or (in the light of new research into human energies in the Soviet Union and the United States) an actual psychic emanation.

At any rate, my telling the woman about my experience, as I did, brought her great solace.

My earliest personal encounter with spiritual healing—healing of the body by the spirit—concerned a small boy in my church school, a victim of hemophilia. He had been suffering from severe chronic throat infections. The doctors were afraid that if they operated, the boy's blood might not clot and death would result. However, if they didn't operate, there was every likelihood the throat infections would kill him.

I took the boy to the regular healing services at St. Stephen's Episcopal Church in Philadelphia. After the fourth visit, his throat infections cleared, and no operation was necessary. The family doctor was impressed, in spite of himself—he couldn't conceive, he said, in terms of his medical knowledge, how so dramatic a physical change could occur in anybody so quickly.

The armchair psychoanalysts, of course, may mutter knowingly about "psychosomatics" and "hysteria," using such words almost as incantations to exorcise any "superstitious" idea that faith really can heal. But I wonder if it is any gain in understanding to glibly attribute every unusual healing to "psychosomatics" instead of, as among our less sophisticated forebears, to "faith." Possibly it's a mere semantic quibble. Isn't the important thing that sick people be healed—whether by pills, by prayer, or by a combination of both?

(The whole question of spiritual and psychic healing, an immensely important one, is considered in Chapter 5.)

Dreams—the "Royal Road to the Unconscious"

Many of my early parishioners reported psychic experiences in the form of dreams—dreams of the future, even compelling dreams of conversations with dead relatives or friends.

This, I soon realized, was no accident, since dreams, Freud's "royal road to the unconscious," lead to those deeper levels of the mind that harbor ESP and other latent human talents. Traditionally, dreams have been the vehicle for communications from angels, spirits, even God. The Bible abounds in psychic dreams.

Remember Pilate's wife who was "much troubled" in her dreams by "this just man," Jesus? Or Joseph and his richly symbolic, magnificently prescient dreams? Or the dream that warned the Wise Men to return to their country by another way to escape Herod's evil machinations?

A remarkable, spiritually meaningful dream was experienced by a parishioner of mine who, after confessing that though he attended church with his wife he never had given much thought to spiritual matters, told me how recently he had been thinking about a friend of his, a coworker who was dead, when the man suddenly appeared.

"I don't know whether I'd fallen asleep or not," this

parishioner said, "but there was Woody, standing in front of me, large as life, smiling.

"He said to me, 'How're you doing, Clayt?' I said, 'Why, Woody, it can't be you. Let me touch you.'

"With that, I put out my hand and he vanished.

"The next day I mentioned what had happened to another guy at work who also was a good friend of Woody's. You know what? He admitted that *he'd* seen Woody, too, and was scared to tell anybody for fear they'd say he was crazy."

In sharing this story, the parishioner concluded: "You know, Father, I never thought much about these things before. But I do now."

What made this case peculiarly interesting was that two men, independently, saw an apparition of the same deceased friend—two men who distinctly were not in the habit of seeing ghosts. Curious about what might have triggered this unusual double apparition (because the two appearances, I felt, definitely were linked), I investigated and found that Woody's wife was very bitter about his passing. She had railed against God, protesting that it wasn't "fair" that her husband was singled out by death.

My intuition was that this woman's bitterness was preventing her husband from progressing in the next life. (After all, if the dead can influence the living, why not vice versa?) Perhaps Woody was trying to tell his wife, through his friends, since her bitterness made it impossible for him to reach her directly, that all was well with him and that she should relinquish her anger and release him from her thoughts.

I detect no faulty theology here but rather a confirmation of the doctrine of the communion of saints—that all God's children, living and dead, are interrelated. If, as many Christians believe, and I personally believe, the prayers of the living can help the dead, why should it not be equally true that the negative thoughts of the living may hinder the dead?

A dream, a lovely spiritual allegory, with precisely this theme was reported to me by a parishioner. She had been bitter for years over the death of a child. One night she dreamed "of a long line of children, all dressed in white and all carrying a candle and walking through a great gate or arch which seemed to be the gate of Heaven.

"My daughter," said the woman, "was in the line—at the very end. She was always at the end. Each time, as I watched her approach the gate, her candle went out. Apparently she couldn't enter the gate unless her candle was lit, and she couldn't keep it lit.

"I called to her, 'Why can't you keep your candle alight?' And in her so-familiar voice she replied, 'Because, mother, your tears keep putting it out.'"

The woman's grief dissolved from that moment and was replaced by a loving, freeing "Godspeed" to her daughter who, after all, simply had gone on before.

Precognitive Experiences

The files of parapsychology bristle with cases of apparitions similar to the one I've described, some perceived in the waking state, some in a dream. And dreams can act as channels for other psychic experiences, too, such as clairvoyance—the perception of a distant event (or its auditory equivalent, clairaudience).

Once, while visiting friends on a short holiday, I half awakened and lay in that state in which images come and go and reality seems half real and half dream. (Psychologists call this the "hypnogogic state.") Suddenly my shifting images were jarred by the voice of my secretary, Verna Schmidt, which cut through my reverie like a knife. I heard clearly and distinctly the words: "You are wanted at Underwood Hospital. There has been an accident and a woman is dying."

I was startled. On a two-day vacation, I was not within easy driving distance of my church, where my secretary was. But the experience of having heard her voice as distinctly as though she were in the room had me on edge, and I left to return home sooner than planned.

Several hours later, when I entered my office in Woodbury, Mrs. Schmidt greeted me with the very words she had spoken in my reverie: "You are wanted at Underwood Hospital. There has been an accident and a woman is dying."

In my absence, she told me, another priest had gone to the hospital.

But how had I heard her voice two hundred miles away?

Dreams may also act as a tunnel to the future. Precognition is an uncanny phenomenon, supremely inscrutable because it transcends time and raises unfathomable questions about the nature of free will and destiny. It occurs too often, however, to be seriously doubted. Sometimes the precognitive experience takes on a spiritual dimension by generating faith in God.

In July 1973 a thirteen-year-old girl who had died tragically was buried. Later I learned that six months earlier the girl had dreamed her own death. This revelation made it easier, somehow, for the girl's mother to bear her grief; as if, pointless though the tragedy seemed, there *were* a point and the strange dream provided a clue to it.

In her dream, the girl died in "a freak accident." In reality, she died after a tractor trailer jumped the curb and crushed her while she walked with her mother near her home. (The mother suffered a broken pelvis in the accident.)

Let's call the girl (whose mother wishes anonymity) Judy. Shortly after Judy's death a friend gave her mother a letter the dead girl had written on December 6, 1972. The letter was eerily prophetic.

Judy wrote to her friend that she dreamed she had been injured in an accident and lay in hopsital near death.

"The doctors said I had only a 30 per cent chance of recovery," the girl wrote.

She described a procession of high school friends who visited her. And then, in the dream, she died.

"From somewhere above me I heard a voice," she wrote, "which said, 'Judy Jones died from a freak accident at the age of thirteen.

"'She had many friends who loved her and still love her now, even though she is no longer with us. They think of her often. When they think of her, they do not think of her untimely death but her short but fulfilled and happy life.'"

Then, in her dream, Judy said she saw and heard a friend telling a group of classmates: "I hope that you won't remember Judy by her death but by her simply super life. And tonight, when you pray to God, remember to ask Him to help us remember Judy."

The letter concluded: "Then the dream ended. Do you think it could be true? Love, Judy."

Six months later, Judy was dead.

The girl's letter is deeply moving. Personally, it is hard for me not to believe that she did glimpse what lay ahead for herself: death at such an early age, the victim of a freak accident.

Perhaps the purpose of the premonitory dream was to prepare her for her death. Though the awareness that it was a death omen apparently never fully crystallized, the thought obviously occurred to her. And at the deep level of her inner self she may well have known perfectly what the dream was all about.

This experience, despite its tragedy, has a luminous

quality. It reminds us that we live surrounded by mysteries, and the most wonderful of all is the human spirit which, though it can be contained in a small body, towers over time and space and death.

Fletcher Predicts

During my first few months in that small parish in Florence, back in 1957, I didn't see Arthur Ford again, nor did I expect to. Then one day in August he appeared, typically unannounced, and in an ebullient mood. Before he left he had given me a trance sitting, my first private meeting with Fletcher.

In that séance, Fletcher said: "Have you ever been called an Italian?"

"Well," I replied, "strangely enough, I was only recently."

Fletcher then described my former college professor George Haupt, gave his name, and said: "He's been doing some checking up on you. He says, Fiorenza . . . you were there."

"I'm in Florence now," I observed.

"We know that," Fletcher responded a trifle impatiently, "but this was in Italy."

Then he proceeded to describe a previous life in which, he said, I had been a follower of the great fifteenth-century Florentine reformer Savonarola. (The subsequent story of some curious links with Savonarola is told in Chapter 11.)

Fletcher made a prediction, still speaking, it seemed, for Haupt: "You will only be here for three years. . . . Where you are going will be a step up for you."

I didn't take the prediction too seriously. Though my church was no Cathedral of St. John the Divine (it seated only fifty people, if they all exhaled), I was content with my munificent salary of three thousand dollars; at least nobody could accuse me of being there for the money.

At the beginning of my third year in Florence my then bishop, the Right Reverend Alfred L. Banyard, visited the parish for confirmation service. As he was preparing to leave, he said, almost as if it were an afterthought: "Bill, there's a church in Woodbury where the rector has been for forty-two years. I think you would do well there. Are you interested?"

With almost indecent haste, I said "Yes."

Later in the year my name was submitted to the vestry of Christ Church, Woodbury. The vestrymen visited me twice, and then I was formally called to be their rector, and accepted.

Some months later the vestry announced that my predecessor as rector was retiring several months before he was originally scheduled to do so. Accordingly, I moved to Woodbury in August 1960. This was, as it happened, *three years to the month* after Arthur Ford's prediction. The change of date made the prediction exactly correct.

Fletcher had been right, after all. But then, as I was to learn, he had a way of being right. . . .

A Psychic Explosion?

When I was treading my early psychic paths, the subject, if not exactly taboo in church circles, was certainly less than popular. Though parapsychology even then had invaded labs and colleges around the world and was winning grudging acceptance from the academic establishment, the subject for churchmen still exuded a whiff of sulphur—and more than a whiff if the churchman was an archconservative, in which case he was likely to denounce any form of psychic investigation as part of the devil's works. More common than the ecclesiastical anathema, however, was the priestly smirk. (One priest, at a diocesan clergy conference, said of a speaker's antipsychic remark: "That ought to fix Rauscher and his ESP shit!")

But all that has changed. Now, twenty years later, the shock waves unleashed by the occult revolution are rocking the churches. Suddenly everybody knows his or her astrological sign. Mediums are going into trance on prime-time television between commercial breaks. Students en masse are consulting the ouija board and the I Ching, doing astral projection, opening their third eye, and ascending to Nirvana by a variety of other routes. These are all manifestations of what *Time* called "the cult of the occult."

Most people in the churches, including the clergy—perhaps especially the clergy—don't know what to make of the psychic wave that threatens to engulf our whole society.

Is it a mere fad, they wonder hopefully, like hoola-hooping or streaking? Is the wisest policy for the Church simply to ignore the whole thing, as one would an embarrassing but harmless attack of the itch?

Or, rather, is the rising occult tide a murky inundation by evil, as some fundamentalist religionists claim? Should the churches be admonishing their faithful to leave everything that pertains to the psychic severely alone?

Or could it be, as a relatively small but growing number of churchmen are saying and no doubt still more are thinking, that the current rediscovery of the occult is an honest attempt by many people to find fresh meaning for their lives? Is the pyschic explosion a symptom of spiritual hunger? And are the churches at least partly responsible for it by having banished mysticism and the "supernatural" from the lexicon of faith? Are there valuable insights that the churches can gain from the psychic?

The latter viewpoint, of course, is the thesis of this

book. Consider with me, in succeeding chapters, such questions as these:

Does the Bible forbid communication with the dead? Should a Christian ever attend séances? Are mediums modern witches and sorcerers, or are they akin, rather, to saints and mystics?

Does telepathy explain prayer, or explain it away? When we pray, are we merely communicating with other human beings via ESP, or are we communicating with God too?

What about descriptions of the next world provided by the best mediums: Do they agree with the Christian concept of the afterlife? What about Heaven and Hell? Purgatory?

Is reincarnation true? Can it be interpreted in such a way as to be compatible with biblical and Church teaching? Why isn't reincarnation in the New Testament—or is it?

Now to get down to some answers. . . .

4

THE BIBLE AND
PSYCHIC
PHENOMENA

When Bishop Pike said he believed he had communicated with his dead son, there were two quite contrasting reactions from religionists. Extremely liberal theologians said that what Pike claimed couldn't be done, while the extremely conservative said that it *shouldn't* be.

This second, do-not-touch attitude is common to fundamentalists, who tend to interpret the Bible literally. They condemn, as a rule, any psychic experience—unless, of course, it happened to them—as a manifestation of the devil.

Fundamentalists of this extreme antipsychic persuasion appear, in fact, to have a devil complex. They discern the wiles of the evil one in virtually everything. If this sort of religionist dislikes a proposal, principle, or practice—it's of the devil. The phrase becomes a smear, used as the word "communist" was during the witch-hunting McCarthy era of the 1950s.

For some religious bigots, to speak bluntly, the phrase

"of the devil" simply means anything they don't happen to agree with. And many don't agree with psychic phenomena, whether in the Church or out of it.

Of course, given the history of ideas, we shouldn't be surprised by such opposition. Every departure from strict conformism, whether the notion that the earth was round, the use of chloroform as an anesthetic, or the theory of biological evolution, has been denounced by knee-jerk religious reactionaries as wrong, evil, diabolical. We should not expect so important and provocative a subject as parapsychology to fare any better.

But what does the Bible really say about psychic phenomena? Does it approve them, disapprove, or discriminate between certain phenomena that are permissible and others that are not?

Is there any uniform biblical viewpoint on paranormal occurrences, or a variety of viewpoints? How authoritative is the Bible in this matter, anyway?

How should an intelligent Christian interpret biblical teaching on ESP, mediums, communication with the dead, and other psychic occurrences?

One basic conception must be clarified: the matter of exactly what the Bible is.

As the word implies, it's not one book but many—a library (the literal sense of "bible"). These books differ according to when and by whom they were written, for what purpose and in what context, and in their literary and ethical levels.

The Scriptures, make no mistake, are no more all of a piece ethically or spiritually than they are linguistically. One biblical book, Esther, doesn't even mention the name of God. Another, Lamentations, purveys a philosophy of abysmal pessimism. Other Old Testament texts support ideas that belong to the period, as one little girl put it, "before God became a Christian."

A Manifestation of the Devil?

Biblical literalists often attack modern mediumship by quoting the injunction in Leviticus: "Thou shalt not suffer a witch to live." Well, leaving aside for the moment the vexed question of precisely what "witch" means, consider that the same book of Scripture also declares that anyone who strikes his mother or father or even curses them, should receive the death penalty (Exod. 21:15, 17), while if he kills his slave he should merely be "punished," and then only if the slave dies immediately, "for he [the slave] is his money." (Exod. 21:20).

Is it really so important whether Leviticus condemns "them that have familiar spirits" (again, applied by critics, debatably, to modern mediums) when we know that the very same Old Testament Scriptures authorize the Israelites to "buy" the children of "strangers" (that is, non-Israelites) to be their "possession" and to be bequeathed to their heirs (Exod. 25:45)?

Moreover, the Jewish Scriptures that fundamentalists cite as decreeing the stoning of witches and wizards also decree the death penalty for anybody who works on the Sabbath (Exod. 31:14); the extermination of a defeated enemy, including every man, woman, and child (I Sam. 15:3); the blessedness of him who smashes the heads of an enemy's children (Ps. 137:9); and the "uncleanness" of any married couple that has sexual intercourse (Lev. 15:18).

My point is that whether a scriptural text allows or disallows a particular practice is not, in itself, a sufficient guide in spiritual matters. If it were, then we should execute people who work on the Sabbath, and we should also restore slavery and hang rebellious sons and daughters.

What the mature Christian seeks in any serious matter is the *substance* of scriptural teaching, the biblical consensus, taking into account all relevant questions such as who said it, when, and why.

Arthur Ford, who as a medium was used to receiving un-Christian abuse from a great many people who called themselves Christians, always professed to be puzzled as to why biblical literalists didn't carry out the Old Testament injunctions to kill witches. His conclusion was that, strangely, these people were at a higher level than the God they professed to believe in because they declined to carry out His bloodthirsty commands.

Actually, the first five books of the Old Testament, upon which the antipsychic attitudes of fundamentalists generally rest, were nothing so much as an attempt to beat the competition being offered to the Mosaic priesthood of that day by a growing number of unorthodox prophets and mediums. The wholesale proscription of wizardry and divination was to prevent anyone from functioning outside the approved religious institutions of the time. In the later books of the Old Testament, and in the New Testament, this blanket proscription is modified considerably.

On the emotion-charged question of the alleged diabolical origin of psychic phenomena, Arthur Ford had some eminently sane words.

"If modern psychic manifestations are all the work of deceiving devils, as some fundamentalists tell us," he said, "how can one be sure that the angels that appeared to the prophets, the apostles, and to Jesus were not all the works of the devil?

"In fact, how can we know that the appearance of Jesus after His death wasn't a deception engineered by the devil?"

Puffing on his cigar and staring quietly out the window for a moment, Ford continued: "Obviously, those disciples who witnessed Jesus' appearances, the 120 who are reported to have seen Him on one occasion, were all people like we are, and just as liable to be victims of deception.

"This whole devil theory is so illogical and destructive of the Christian position that one marvels at the stupidity of those who use it. If the so-called dead cannot be seen and identified by the living today, then there is no certainty that Jesus ever identified Himself to His disciples after His death on the cross."

It's noteworthy that Jesus had to meet and answer the same devil argument, which, in every age, it seems, is trotted out by religious reactionaries who prefer their familiar darkness to new light. When his critics, the pious, orthodox religionists of that day, accused Jesus of casting out devils with the aid of the prince of devils, He replied: "If I, by Beelzebub cast out demons [which in Greek, by the way, means "familiar spirits"], by whom do your sons cast them out? Therefore shall they be your judges." (Luke 11:19).

Jesus' point was well taken. If today's psychic events, which parallel many in the Bible, are all the works of the devil who, then, was responsible for the biblical wonders? The modern Pharisees, who attribute everything they don't understand nor want to understand to the devil, are guilty of the same sin as Jesus' accusers.

If healing is of God when it comes through a Pentecostal evangelist, a priest laying on hands, or a shrine such as Lourdes, isn't it just as much "of God" when it comes, and it does, through a Spiritualist medium or, for that matter, a Christian Science practitioner? One does not need to approve everything about a person to appreciate him as an instrument of God. As a priest of the Episcopal Church, I certainly reject many of the precepts of Spiritualism and Christian Science, but it would be both wicked and foolish of me to deny that

God works through people within these movements and others.

Healing is healing. God's work is God's work. And bringing hope to the hopeless is God's work, no matter who does it.

"Can Satan," demanded St. Paul, "cast out Satan?" Can the devil, the evil one, the father of lies, really be the author of psychic experiences which, to my certain knowledge, have made people morally and spiritually better, more truthful, and more loving?

With evidence, I'm prepared to accept just about anything, but to expect me to believe that the devil has gone into God's business by restoring people to health and goodness is to ask an act of faith of which I personally am incapable.

The Psychic Stream in the Bible

Looked at objectively, putting religious bias aside, the Bible abounds in experiences identical, outwardly at least, to those we now call psychic phenomena.

In the Old Testament there are plenteous accounts: *ESP* (in II Kings 6, the prophet Elisha discerns the secret plans of the king of Syria); *psychokinesis* or *mind over matter* (in the same chapter, Elisha makes iron swim in water); *prophetic dreams* (in Gen. 28, the dream of Jacob's ladder); *levitation* (in II Kings 2, Elijah whirls up in a chariot of fire); and *communication with the dead* (in I Sam. 28, Saul contacts the dead Samuel with the aid of the Woman of Endor).

Old Testament examples of psychic phenomena could be multiplied almost endlessly. But more important, the New Testament, especially the Gospels, teems with similar accounts.

Jesus, of course, healed the sick, but He also walked

on water (*levitation*), multiplied the loaves and fishes (*psychokinesis*), prophesied his death and Resurrection (*precognition*), read other people's thoughts (*extrasensory perception*), mysteriously disappeared out of the midst of a hostile crowd (so-called *teleportation*), and communicated with the dead.

Yes, Jesus communicated with the dead. On the Mount of Transfiguration, in the company of Peter, James, and John, He saw and conversed with Moses and Elijah, long dead. The disciples, who also saw and heard the two prophets' spirit forms, were so awed that they wanted to build a shrine on the spot.

This incident, you could say, was the only séance conducted by Jesus Himself.

There is no phenomenon reported in the Gospels, with the exception of the raising of Lazarus from the dead and, of course, the Resurrection of Christ Himself, that is not encountered outside the pages of the Bible.

The great medium D. D. Home was levitated in the presence of scientists such as Sir William Crookes, and on one occasion floated out one upstairs window of a London house and back in another.

The contemporary Israeli psychic Uri Geller, though still controversial, is accredited by reputable scientists as having performed astonishing feats of mind over matter; in my presence he apparently zapped a gold ring, psychically, so that it bent, and my church key broke in pieces inside his cupped hands.

Subjects in the Menninger Dream Lab at Brooklyn's Maimonides Medical Center repeatedly have demonstrated the ability to pick up, in their dreams, other people's thoughts, and even future events.

Numerous psychics I've known, such as Arthur Ford, Eileen Garrett, Jeane Dixon, Douglas Johnson, and Ena Twigg, have read my mind, described distant events (called *clairvoyance*), correctly probed my future, and, on occasion, conveyed information that seemed convincingly to have come from the dead.

Throughout Church history, before the word "parapsychology" was invented, similar experiences were going on. They were rampant in the lives of the saints: Joseph of Copertino flew like a bird, St. Philip Neri was illuminated by a preternatural light, St. Teresa of Avila saw visions and heard voices, and St. Alphonse Ligouri experienced being in two places at once (called *bilocation* or, by occultists, "astral projection").

And Protestant mystics and evangelists experienced similar things. John Wesley, founder of Methodism, for example, had frequent communications from the dead, sometimes spontaneously ("In dreams," he wrote in his *Journal,* "I have had exceeding lively conversation with them") and sometimes through pious mediums, such as a woman named Elizabeth Hobson. In one account Wesley describes how on the death of Miss Hobson's brother in Jamaica he (the brother) appeared at her bedside in England.

"A spirit finds no difficulty in travelling three thousand or four thousand miles in a moment," remarked Wesley.

There is, then, a psychic stream in the Bible, and it has continued to flow through the lives of Christians down through the ages. To have a psychic experience, or to seek one, is no more un-Christian than to have or to seek, for example, a sexual relationship. Whether the latter is right or wrong is a moral and ethical judgment, and the value of a psychic experience must be similarly judged.

For What Purpose, Psychic Phenomena?

Though Jesus performed healing miracles, stilled storms, and even raised the dead, He never did these as mere stunts, as things to be valued for their own sake. He discouraged miracle mongering and, in fact, in the Temptation narrative, rejected any such inclination as "tempting" God.

What made Jesus' miracles more than mere psychic oddities, however amazing, was that the working of them was motivated by His love for God and man. Thus they became signs of God's love to an unbelieving world. Miracles.

This, then, is the mature biblical perspective on psychic phenomena: They are welcome as manifestations of God's universe, as wonderful as any of its profound mysteries, to be spiritualized by faith and love.

To say whether psychic experiences are good, pleasing to God, is as easy, and as difficult, as to say whether sex is pleasing to God. In Christian marriage, sex is a sacrament ("the outward and visible sign of an inward and spiritual grace"); in rape it is a violation.

Similarly, if psychic abilities are used to help and to heal people, they are good. However, if such powers are misused, turned against others or oneself through ignorance or malice, they are bad.

I know people—some of their cases will be discussed in the chapter on psychic problems—whose lives have been marred by an unwise, unholy tampering with psychic forces. Nervous breakdowns, insanity, states of borderline or even real possession—these can and have been known to follow an unhealthy dabbling in the occult.

On the other hand, I've seen shattered faith put back together by someone's experience of talking to a deceased wife or husband through a medium. Lives have been saved—physically, in some cases—by psychic warnings. Bodies have been healed by psychic means after medical science gave up. Trust in God and in Christ has been renewed by the comfort of sensing, knowing, that a dead loved one is alive and near; that human life goes beyond death; and that miracles, thank God, haven't ceased.

5

HEALING
Prayers or Pills?

Olga Worrall is a faith healer even doctors believe in.

The respected professional publication *Medical Economics*, in a profile of this grandmotherly Baltimore woman who has been practicing spiritual and psychic healing for forty years, quoted praise for her from several physicians.

Said Dr. Robert Bradley, a Denver gynecologist: "I've known of Olga Worrall over a number of years and I've come to the conclusion that she's a sincere person with a decided gift for healing."

Dr. Paul G. Isaak, a family physician in Alaska, remarked of Mrs. Worrall as a healer: "I must say that I am favorably impressed."

Dr. William McGary, director of an Arizona clinic, commented: "Olga Worrall has a remarkable ability to heal."

And Dr. James A. Knight, associate dean and professor of psychiatry at Tulane University Medical School, declared: "I view Mrs. Worrall's healing ministry with enthusiasm and confidence."

And what does this chatty, sixtyish healer, who calls

everybody "Honey" (as an old friend she's been calling me that for years) have to say for herself?

"Don't call me a miracle worker," she requests. "I simply channel to the afflicted a primal healing power that flows from God. God is the healer, not me. So-called miracles are the working out of the laws of God on a higher level than we understand."

Olga, who accepts no money for her healing work, for many years has conducted spiritual healing services at Baltimore's Mount Washington Methodist Church. On occasion she has conducted healing services in my parish, and once, functioning as the medium, she held a séance there.

Olga is the widow of an aeronautical engineer, also a dear friend of mine, who had a reputation in his own right as healer and psychic. Ambrose Worrall went everywhere with his wife as half of a unique healing team. Since his death in 1972 she still signs her letters to friends: "Ambrose and Olga."

What sort of cases respond to Olga Worrall's brand of spiritual therapy?

Olga Worrall Heals

Gai Washington, whose mother runs a Baltimore nursing home, was born with severe brain damage, and by the age of four was deaf, blind, and suffering from a serious heart condition. Her brain, according to the report in *Medical Economics*, was so extensively destroyed that doctors described her head as virtually an empty shell.

Mrs. Washington took her daughter to an Olga Worrall healing service, where she received the laying on of hands with prayer. The child was taken to such services many times over a period of years. She gradually improved to the point where today she's described as a normal schoolgirl.

Coincidence? A freakish remission of symptoms? Or the delayed result of medical treatment?

Well, a doctor who knew the case well said he didn't believe "medical treatment alone could have saved the girl."

In another case, a Baltimore boy, Jeffrey Kenney, suffered from a crippling bone disease that doctors said would disable him permanently. Mrs. James Kenney took her son to Olga Worrall for prayer and the laying on of hands. Today the boy no longer wears his leg brace and appears perfectly normal.

Of this case, a doctor said cautiously: "Recovery did occur where, medically, it was not logically expected to occur." He added that the cure "might have" been the result of "sheer willpower" on the boy's part.

Olga Worrall says she isn't fussy who gets the credit as long as a sick person gets well. She has excellent relations with doctors, and encourages people who come for healing always to continue their medical treatment until such time as it becomes obvious they no longer need it.

Thus, Olga avoids the dangerous practice—and one for which some faith healers are justly criticized by the medical profession—of encouraging or even exhorting people to throw away their medications and simply "have faith."

Telling a desperately sick person to simply "have faith," Olga Worrall no doubt would agree, makes no more sense than telling a motorist with a flat tire to have faith. In both cases obviously something more than simple faith is needed.

Because of her sensible, rational approach to healing, and her promedical attitude, Olga frequently finds doctors among those who come to her for prayer.

"One night," she recalled with a chuckle, "there were nine M.D.s—count 'em—in the house, all seeking spiritual therapy for their own ailments."

In a field that is riddled, alas, with extremism, fantasy,

and outright fraud, Olga Worrall comes on like perfect sanity—cool, soft-spoken, reasonable, yet compassionate.

"The thing that permitted miracles to happen two thousand years ago is still around," she says so calmly that it's hard not to believe her, "if only we would make use of it."

My friend Olga Worrall represents the kind of healing ministry with which the Church should be identified. She avoids the false and mischievous separation that some healers make between penicillin and prayer—as though one were any less from God than the other—and stresses that doctors and priests, medical and spiritual practitioners, ought to work together to heal man in soul, mind, and body.

What Are the Dangers in Faith Healing?

There can be no legitimate criticism of the Church's healing ministry—directed toward the cure of physical as well as spiritual ills, sickness as well as sin—if always, as in Olga Worrall's case, certain safeguards are observed.

For example, there must never be any implication that an individual is sick because God is punishing him; that disease is somehow a judgment for sin. This is not to say that a physical illness may not be rooted in causes that have a spiritual aspect; alcoholism, for example, which can destroy a man's health, certainly has a spiritual aspect. But the recognition that spiritual malaise can influence the mind and body and contribute to physical sickness is a far cry from the simple-minded idea that God sends people cancer to punish them.

The unpardonable sin of some faith healers, usually of the revivalist type, is to set up the utterly false equation that if "having faith" means being healed, then not being healed must mean not having faith. The result is that if the seeker isn't healed in body, he goes away much worse off than before, because now, in addition to being sick, he believes it's his fault. His lack of faith prevented the healing. In many cases the result of such tragic misguidance has been spiritual shipwreck.

Of course, from the faith healer's point of view, it's great psychology: If a patient gets cured, the healer takes the credit; if not, the patient takes the blame.

Another danger in faith healing, as I intimated earlier, is the utterly false distinction between "faith" and "works." If you're going to trust God for healing, say some healers, you must trust Him totally. That means giving up your medicine.

But this makes no more sense than to say that if you're going to trust God when you travel, trust him all the way and just forget about the car or plane. Simply have faith. The only reason why this latter example seems any more farfetched than the first is fuzzy thinking. Using medicine when you're sick is about as much sign of lack of faith as taking the plane to get from New York to Los Angeles, instead of trusting angels to whisk you there.

When a healer, such as Olga Worrall, embraces, on the one hand, all that medicine has to offer and, on the other, the resources of faith and prayer that the Church has to offer, who can criticize such a ministry?

In healing, as in every other aspect of the psychic world, there is diversity. No two healers are identical. Often they disagree, sometimes sharply, on matters of practice or even of faith. But all are doing God's work.

Spectacularly different from Olga Worrall in many ways, yet profoundly like her in the essence of her healing ministry, is the noted evangelist Kathryn Kuhlman.

Of all the healing services I have attended, the most impressive and remarkable was at the First Presbyterian Church, Pittsburgh, on a Friday morning in July 1970. The service was scheduled to start at 11 A.M. but, because the church was jammed with three thousand people an hour before that, the proceedings started early.

When Kathryn Kuhlman appeared, a tall, striking figure in white silk, the congregation greeted her with a tumult of applause. The air was thick with love. And expectancy.

From a psychic standpoint, a Kathryn Kuhlman "miracle service" (as she calls it) is an astonishing performance. Not only are there the healings themselves—cataracts dropping from eyes, shriveled limbs visibly lengthened, palpable tumors regressing out of existence—but there is an incredible display of what might be called medical clairvoyance.

Kathryn Kuhlman, an unreconstructed Baptist, doesn't call it that. She says simply: "The Spirit tells me." But what the Spirit tells her about some of the people in that vast congregation is astonishingly accurate, matching the feats of the greatest psychics.

"There's someone in the fifth row, downstairs, who's being healed of an arthritic hand. It's your left hand. That's right. Move your fingers. You can do it now!"

Or: "Up in the balcony, near the back, the second-to-last row, there's a woman with varicose veins being healed. Your left leg was worse. The veins are healed."

Or: "At the back on the ground floor, over here on my left, there's somebody, a man, with a tumor that's just disappeared. It was behind your left knee when you came in. The size of an orange. Feel it now. It's gone!"

Incredibly, in almost every case the person later comes to the platform and acknowledges that the evangelist correctly diagnosed his or her condition, as well as divining the fact of healing.

That inexplicable cures do occur in Kathryn Kuhlman's meetings seems beyond any dispute, reasonable or otherwise. (For documented examples, see Allen Spraggett's *Kathryn Kuhlman: The Woman Who Believes in Miracles*, New York: The World Publishing Company,

1970.) Some are so strange as to rival the most spectacular in the Bible.

Is Kathryn Kuhlman a Saint?

One of the strangest purported healings involved a man named George Davis. On September 23, 1971, at the age of forty-eight, he had a serious heart attack. He spent two months in the hospital, and when he came out he had a pacemaker—a small mechanical device that keeps the heartbeat normal—sewn into his body. The pacemaker, for the record, was surgically inserted on November 4, 1972.

Nine months later, Davis attended a miracle service in Pittsburgh, felt a sudden surge of heat rush through his body, and fainted (or swooned—nobody knows what it is, but it happens to many in Kathryn Kuhlman's meetings).

Instead of feeling well when he regained consciousness, however, as most people do after being "struck by The Power" (as the Kuhlmanites call it), George Davis felt weird, ill, groggy. On the way home to nearby Donora, Pennsylvania, in his father's car, he fell into a profound sleep.

Later, when he took a shower, he noticed that the scar where the pacemaker had been inserted in his chest had disappeared. He rushed to the doctors and, upon examining him, they scratched their heads and confirmed it: The scar was gone. Not only that—*the pacemaker was gone too!*

Fantastic? Impossible?

Of course. But when a reporter for the Pittsburgh *Press* contacted the physician who treated the man after his heart attack, Dr. George Johnston of Philadelphia said, yes, Davis did have a pacemaker inserted and, no, he didn't have it any more.

"I can confirm that he had a heart attack," Dr. Johnston reportedly said of his patient, "that a pacemaker was placed in his body, and that now the pacemaker and the five-inch incision scar are gone."

All this was a simple matter of record, said the doctor. But an explanation? Well, that was something that neither he nor any other doctor has attempted.

After attending the miracle service, I spent an hour privately with Kathryn Kuhlman. To my mind, she's totally dedicated to God and totally uninterested in trying to analyze, dissect, or explore rationally what happens in her meetings. She's not well disposed toward being asked whether she's psychic, clairvoyant, or has ESP. She is or has all these things, of course, but for her the healing phenomenon and what is associated with it are simply the fruit of "the spirit of God."

Kathryn Kuhlman's theological background leaves little room, if any, for a consideration of how her experiences fit into the universal patterns of psychic phenomena. And who cares? Certainly not I. When cancers are shriveling and crooked legs being straightened, to argue about theology or parapsychology would be absurdly trivial. The towering fact about Kathryn Kuhlman is that enormous psychic gifts, consecrated to God, have become the channel for true miracles that glorify Jesus Christ.

The key to Kathryn Kuhlman is her utter dedication to her spiritual ministry.

"When you give yourself to God without any reservation whatsoever—without any reservation whatsoever, you hear," she told me, "body, soul, mind, and spirit; when you hold nothing back; when you surrender the works; when you say, and mean it, 'Lord I am yours, use me'— then, brother, things happen!"

Is Kathryn Kuhlman a saint?

Only God knows. But I have a suspicion about His feelings on the matter.

What is the power, the energy, at work in medically unexplained healings such as those of Olga Worrall and Kathryn Kuhlman?

Kathryn Kuhlman is content to call it simply "the power of God" and discourages probing deeper. Yet solar radiation could be called, in a sense, the power of God, as can electricity and other natural forces. Is it possible to go beyond a statement of faith (which is what the expression "the power of God" really is) to a more precise, more analytic formulation?

What is the nature, for example, of this particular power of God? How can it possibly act so differently at different times—here, shriveling a tumor; there, melting a cataract, regenerating a dead nerve, or causing a shattered bone to be restored to wholeness?

How is the healing force generated? By prayer? The use of the sacraments? Hymn singing? By faith alone?

Can anybody produce or channel it, or only special people? If the latter, what makes such people special? Is healing a skill that can be acquired, or a gift, to be developed if it's present?

It is in offering answers, however provisional, to questions such as these that parapsychology comes to the aid of theology. A number of provocative scientific experiments have shed welcome light on such questions.

The Power of Healing Force—Dr. Bernard Grad's Experiment

A Presbyterian minister-chemist, Franklin Loehr, some twenty years ago opened up a fruitful new avenue for psychic research when he conducted a series of experiments with prayer and plants. He found, after making twenty-eight thousand measurements of barley seedlings, that when the plants were subjected to identical treat-

ment, except that some received prayer while the others
didn't, the prayed-over ones grew significantly better.

Loehr's work, published as a book, *The Power of Prayer
on Plants,* led a scientist at Montreal's McGill University,
Dr. Bernard Grad, to try the same thing himself. Grad
used the prayers of a self-styled healer named Oskar
Estebany. In a slight variation on Loehr's work, he had
the healer pray not for the seedlings themselves but for
a saline solution (water with 1 per cent salt added),
which was then dumped on the plants.

Grad's results, achieved under careful controls and in
not one but a series of experiments, yielded conclusive
evidence that, in his words, "prayer can stimulate cell
growth in plants."

Later Grad added the words "and animals." That was
after he did experiments in which Mr. Estebany and
others were able to speed up the healing of surgical
wounds in laboratory mice by "praying" for the mice.

In an informative twist on the original plant experiments, Grad used morbidly depressed people as pray-ers
and found that they significantly *inhibited* the growth
of seedlings.

Black magic? Well, maybe. At any rate, Grad said he
now had equally strong evidence for the growth-stimulat-
ing power of positive thought, or prayer, and the growth-
inhibiting effect of negative thought, or, if you like, anti-
prayer.

He came to these conclusions: Prayer is a *state of being*
in which people generate an actual force. This force is
not physical or chemical—like sweat or breath—but apparently a form of radiation. The force has two polarities,
positive and negative, depending on the state of mind of
the individual generating it.

Conducted at a great university, under appropriate
blind and double-blind conditions, Grad's work is too
impressive to be dismissed by anyone. Moreover, it wasn't

long before his findings, in substance, were replicated by another scientist in another lab.

A Nun-Scientist Examines Psychic Phenomena

This was Sister Justa Smith, a Franciscan nun, then chairman of the Natural Sciences Department at Rosary Hill College, Buffalo. She is a biochemist with her doctorate in the field of the study of enzymes.

Hearing of Bernard Grad's research, and wanting to confirm or disprove it, Sister Justa decided on a series of experiments in her special field, enzymology.

Enzymes are the substances, sometimes called the "brains" of the cells, that regulate all our vital bodily processes. It's an enzyme in the brain that makes memory possible, another enzyme that enables us to digest our food, still another that controls the level of energy-producing glucose in the bloodstream, and so on.

If some people actually have the power to affect another's bodily health by prayer or the laying on of hands, thought Sister Justa, the effect should show up first as a change in enzyme activity.

In her first experiment Sister Justa tested Grad's healer, Mr. Estebany, using a common enzyme called trypsin, which controls the body's ability to digest protein. For seventy-five minutes each day for eleven days the healer, while in a "prayerful" state of mind, held in his hand a sealed flask containing the enzyme. Each time he significantly stimulated the enzyme's activity. This stimulation was of the same magnitude as would have resulted from exposure of the enzyme for a much longer period to a powerful magnetic field.

It was, said Sister Justa, as though Mr. Estebany's hands were strong magnets. Could the healing energy be a form of biomagnetism?

Well, that was a possibility. But a subsequent experiment showed that it was too simple an answer.

In the case of the first enzyme used, trypsin, a speeding up of its activity in the body—such as was achieved by the healer—would serve to increase the body's ability to assimilate protein, and this, Sister Justa knew, would contribute to the individual's greater health and well-being. But what would happen, she wondered, if the healer tried to influence a different enzyme—one, say, that under certain conditions is too active and, for greater bodily health and well-being, should be slowed down?

If a healer were asked to "pray" over such an enzyme, without being told its properties, would the enzyme's activity speed up, as the trypsin's did, or slow down? Or stay the same way?

And what would be the effect on still another type of enzyme which, for optimum bodily health, should neither increase nor decrease its activity but simply remain stable?

To find the answers, the nun-scientist used three self-styled psychic healers. They repeated precisely what Mr. Estebany had done previously, except that the enzyme used was one called NAD. It affects bodily metabolism and, in the case of a sick person, a *decrease* in its activity would contribute to better health.

The results of this test?

All three healers brought about *reduced* activity of the NAD, without having been told that this was the desired effect. The healing force appeared to "know" whether an enzyme should be stimulated or retarded for optimum health.

In a third experiment, Sister Justa used an enzyme called amylase-amylose, which controls the release of glucose into the bloodstream. Any increase in this enzyme's activity could cause diabetes, while a decrease could cause the opposite: low blood sugar. For optimum health, this enzyme should remain at a stable level of activity. The samples used were taken from the three healers' own blood serum.

The results: as desired, no detectable change in the rate of activity of the amylase-amylose.

Sister Justa's research has far-reaching implications for medicine and religion. It provides another body of evidence that "healing hands" are fact. Human thought and feeling can generate, or at least channel, a force that heals. And, in its positive, creative form, this force is exquisitely selective in its effect on specific bodily processes, which effect is always in the direction of optimum health.

Dr. Grad's use of water as a medium by which the prayer force was conveyed to the barley seedlings—he had the healer pray over a saline solution, remember, which was then dumped on the seeds—brings to the fore holy water and the question of the sacraments as channels of healing.

The Holy Water of Lourdes

There is evidence, interestingly confirmed by Grad's experiments, that at Lourdes, where remarkable cures have occurred, the medium of healing, in most cases at least, is the water. Not that there is anything medicinal in the spring water at the shrine—there isn't. Repeated chemical tests have shown it to be indistinguishable from other spring water in that vicinity. However, could there be something else, something nonphysical, that gives Lourdes water special healing virtue?

The noted British physician and Christian healer, Christopher Woodard, says experiments at the University of Naples and elsewhere showed that injections of Lourdes water contaminated with deadly germs did not harm guinea pigs, whereas injections of contaminated ordinary water were lethal to them. In such cases, the germs in the Lourdes water were not destroyed but simply made nontoxic. Something in the water renders germs inert.

My guess is that over the long years that pilgrims have visited Lourdes, the place has been charged by the tremendous healing energy of millions of prayers. The water is psychically radiocative.

What, then, about holy water used in the sacrament of baptism and other rites of the Church? Does something real, something measurable happen to it when the prayers of blessing are said? Are unknown but powerful forms of energy released?

Consider the strange story of the giant cannas.

There are two groups of canna bulbs involved. One was planted some seven years ago in the rectory flower bed in Woodbury, and at the same time a few extra bulbs were planted in the side yard of the church under the sacristy window.

Canna bulbs are very sensitive to cold and normally are removed from the garden at the end of summer, stored indoors for the winter, and replanted in the spring. A standard text, Taylor's Encyclopedia of Gardening, says: "Over most sections of the United States cannas must be grown as summer bedding plants, as they are tropical plants that will not tolerate frost. In parts of California and the deep South, however, they may be left in the ground."

Well, New Jersey is not California or the Deep South. Accordingly, the canna bulbs in front of the rectory are removed every fall and replanted in the spring. During the summer they are watered every day by the gardener. By contrast, the bulbs outside the sacristy receive no care. They are never removed from the soil and have endured the frost and snow of six winters.

Yet the remarkable fact is that these neglected cannas grow to more than three times the height of the pampered ones. By the end of the summer those in the rectory garden are a mere one and one half to two feet tall, while the others are seven feet or more.

A local florist, Donald Sanderson, said: "It is most unusual that the bulbs have even survived through past winters, let alone flourished."

Why the dramatic difference between the two groups of plants?

In the light of parapsychological research it may be significant that the superior cannas are in a spot where they receive the flow from a special sink in which is disposed the blessed water from baptisms and from the cruets used for holy communion. The holy water flows from a pipe directly on the soil in which these cannas grow.

Is the holy water what makes the difference? Does it carry an energy that enables the cannas, contrary to all gardening lore, not only to survive but to flourish?

The idea that holy water may be impregnated with an actual healing force, that it is in a sense prayer in solution, has nothing to do with a superstitious, magical view of the sacraments but everything to do with the hard, empirical evidence.

The data of parapsychology lend reassuring support to the Church's faith that the sacraments, in ways which, though becoming clearer, ultimately elude our rational understanding, are actual channels of healing.

It is no magical ceremony, nor a mere empty gesture, when a priest, believing, anoints the sick one with oil and lays on hands for healing. It is a sanctified means by which mighty creative forces may be mobilized and unleashed on the sufferer's behalf. The sacrament will always have a spiritual effect, but it may also have a physical one. Parapsychology, as well as theology, says that "the prayer of faith shall save the sick."

But apart from unusual and dramatic cures—which, truth to tell, happen only occasionally—how is the Church's healing mission being fulfilled? If a priest or any believer does not see, in answer to his prayers, the lame walking and the blind seeing, does this mean that the prayers are fruitless?

Are Prayers and Pills Contradictory?

There is a growing body of evidence, from medical sources, that pills and prayers belong together. And even where there is no dramatic cure, the evidence indicates that prayers for healing have a measurable influence. Accordingly, more and more doctors are prescribing prayer as well as penicillin for their patients.

One of them is Dr. Platon Collipp, chief of pediatrics at the Nassau County Medical Center in New York. He set up an experiment using two groups of young people with acute leukemia, the cancerlike disease of the blood. One, made up of ten patients, served as the experimental group; the other, with eight patients, was the control group. The names of the first group were given to ten families in a prayer circle composed of the doctor's friends. Each family received the name of one leukemia patient for whom they were to pray daily over a fifteen-month period. The control group received no such prayers.

To rule out the possibility of suggestion, Dr. Collipp did not tell any of the leukemia patients that they were being prayed for. (It is a known medical fact, you see, that as many as 40 per cent of patients will improve after receiving a placebo, a dummy pill, which they believe to be potent medicine.)

Of the ten patients who received daily prayer, seven were still alive after fifteen months. Of the eight who

were not prayed for, only two were alive after the same period.

A statistical analysis of these results, said Dr. Collipp, showed that there was a 90 per cent chance that the difference between the two groups was due to prayer, or only a 10 per cent chance that it was sheer coincidence.

"My opinion is that the results of this experiment support the view that prayer is efficacious," the physician concluded.

Further support for the value of healing prayer as an adjunct of therapy comes from another doctor who claims to have had unusual success treating cancer by a combination of medicine and meditation.

Meditation is a form of contemplative prayer. Some have defined it as "high prayer," a state in which the individual asks nothing but tries to attune himself to God, the Cosmic Mind, the Source of harmony, beauty, and order, or however he may conceive of the ultimate reality.

Dr. O. Carl Simonton, an Air Force major who is chief of radiation therapy at California's Travis Air Force Base, teaches his cancer patients to put themselves into the meditative state and then "talk" to their body, encouraging it to destroy the cancer and return to normal health. Three times a day the patient is supposed to meditate and visualize himself well and strong. All the while he continues to receive standard medical treatment.

In some cases, says the doctor, this union of medicine and meditation brings results that medicine alone couldn't have achieved.

In one case a sixty-one-year-old man with advanced cancer of the throat was given only a 5 per cent chance of survival. He received radiation therapy and also meditated regularly, visualizing himself as well and strong. Two years later, contrary to the medical prognosis, he was doing fine and appeared to be cancer-free.

Dr. Simonton's view is that cancer is basically due to a

breakdown in the body's immunological defense system. Such a breakdown, he suggests, may be traced to negative states of mind—deep despair, hopelessness, or a death wish.

Deep despair? Hopelessness? A death wish? The ultimate answer to these is faith in God. Arm a patient with faith, and his body may "miraculously" turn back the tide of disease and death.

6

GHOSTS
AND POLTERGEISTS

Many people don't believe in ghosts but, as a certain skeptic said of himself, if he ever saw one, he would be scared to death!

Not all ghosts are unfriendly; the traditional lore has accounts of amiable spirits, besides the more familiar antisocial sort. There are even some who haunt churches and monasteries—holy ghosts, as it were.

What is a ghost?

The question is rather like asking: What's an animal? Animals come in all shapes and sizes, as mammals, birds, fish, and reptiles (as well as the duck-billed platypus, that oddity that doesn't fit in anywhere), and range in appearance from the cuddlesome calf or bear cub to the fearsome crocodile or boa constrictor. Ghosts are similarly diverse.

Theology needs the assistance of parapsychology in delineating the anatomy of ghosts. Up to now, theologians have not quite totally ignored the subject, but have come close. St. Thomas Aquinas, the "angelic doctor," was one theologian who pondered the subject, especially the matter of spectral appearances. He decided that when an apparition of someone manifests, the dead person himself probably is not aware of it (a view shared by some modern parapsychologists). Medieval demonology, on which there is a considerable literature, was in part, I suppose, an attempt to account for certain phenomena that today are regarded as "ghostly" rather than "demonic"—objects flying around the room, bottles frantically popping their corks, and weird sounds, such as scratchings, thumps, and raps.

The Ghost Who Wore an Eisenhower Jacket

These latter phenomena are characterized by parapsychologists as "poltergeist" symptoms, a poltergeist (as distinct from the classic spook) being defined, loosely, as a ghost who haunts a person rather than a place.

Let us examine some authentic cases of haunting, both classic and poltergeist, and consider what parapsychology and informed Christian theology have to say about them, including how to evict a troublesome intruder.

Since ghosts all have such a bad, though sometimes undeserved, reputation, here is a case about a priest and his family and their not unfriendly spectral guest.

The Reverend Harry Collins, his wife, Joan, and their three children live in the vicarage of St. Stephen's Episcopal Church in Mullica Hill, a small New Jersey town where Father Collins has been parish priest since 1968. Ever since they moved into the vicarage, peculiar things have happened.

"Nothing much at first," Joan Collins told me. "We noticed that the tablecloth in the dining room was folded back, accordion style, when none of us had done it. This happened repeatedly when my husband and I were out, or when we were all asleep, or when we were all out and the house was empty and locked up.

"Then we frequently found the end cushion on the sofa moved into a position that suggested somebody had been sleeping and using it as a pillow. For a while I shrugged this off as probably being due to our two cats. But after the cats left, it continued."

There was a year and a half of these unspectacular but nonetheless puzzling incidents before Act Two started.

The inexplicable smells came.

"We noticed a strong aroma pervading parts of the house," said Father Collins. "It was a spicy, pleasant odor, hard to identify.

"Besides my wife and me, our fifteen-year-old son smelled it, and he suggested, 'It's like one of those mosquito candles.' This was significant. Previously my wife and I had agreed between ourselves that the smell was like citronella, which of course is a mosquito repellent. Not an identical smell, but close to it."

The smell was localized in the living room and dining room. The Collinses speculated that possibly humidity was releasing odors from the plaster of the walls. But then another, quite different, smell came.

"This one was so strong there was no mistaking it," said Joan Collins. "Like coffee perking and bacon cooking. It seemed to come from the kitchen and waft through the whole house."

The odd phenomena reached a climax when Harry Collins saw—well, let him tell it.

"The date was March 6, 1971. Another couple had dropped in for a visit in the evening, and we were all in the kitchen when I looked up and saw it standing in the hallway leading to the dining room.

"It was the figure of a man. He had muddy blond hair but his features were indistinct, as though they were in shadow. He was wearing an Eisenhower jacket, and his hands were shoved deep into the slit pockets.

"The figure was perfectly distinct and solid-looking down to the knees, but below that it trailed off so that I could see the floorboards through where the legs should have been."

As the clergyman stared at the figure, dumfounded, it faded away like a television image when the set is switched off. By the time he had alerted his companions, it was gone.

Father Collins' reaction?

"Well, I knew I had seen something uncanny, but there was nothing threatening about it. I didn't feel a chill invade the room or anything at all like that."

A year later came Joan Collins' turn to meet the uninvited visitor.

"I was cleaning a downstairs closet one morning," she recalled, "when suddenly I felt what I can describe only as a sense of presence. I turned and found myself staring at the figure of a man no more than five feet from me. He looked so solid and lifelike that for a moment I thought he must be a flesh-and-blood intruder.

"He appeared to be in his early twenties, with light brown, shaggy hair, wearing an Eisenhower jacket, and military pants. The jacket and pants were a drab olive color.

"Suddenly, as I watched, he became transparent and just faded away."

Having no previous experience with ghosts, the Collinses are short on theories about the identity of their unbidden guest or why he is there. But the family has grown rather to accept the gentle haunting.

This may be a case of what parapsychologists call "place memories," or "psychometric" haunting. Let me explain.

Haunting—the Projection of Images from the Past

Psychometry is the art by which a medium, or other psychically gifted person, handling an object, can tune in on its history; as though the object had a memory and, somehow, the medium can tap that memory. I've sat with psychics, who excel at this sort of thing, such as Britain's Douglas Johnson, and heard them produce startling information about the present, or previous owners, of an object.

Now, keeping in mind this notion of memories adhering to an object, such as a watch, a pen, or a wedding ring, can you see how they might adhere to a house? Such place memories, activated in some manner that we don't understand, could manifest to the occupants of the house as visions, sounds, or, in the Collinses' case, smells.

Such a haunting amounts to the projection of images from the past (including "images" of sounds and smells) on a sort of etheric television screen—not unlike astral reruns of "I Love Lucy."

There are, mind you, credulous people who imagine that every creak, every unexplained closing of a door is a sign of unseen presences, and such cases obviously are not what I'm talking about. There exist, however, too many of the type reported by the Collinses—apparitions with multiple witnesses, inexplicable sounds, peculiar odors, and an indefinable but nevertheless real sense of "presence"—to try to explain them all away as fantasy.

By this concept, every house, of course, is "haunted"— occupied by the memories of events, happy or unhappy, that have taken place within it. Problems seem to occur when these past events include explosions, or, even more likely, repressed smolderings, of emotions such as rage, hate, lust, and, particularly, anguish. According to the late, great psychoanalyst-ghost hunter Nandor Fodor, memories of anguish are most commonly associated with sinister or malevolent hauntings. In such cases, the house is pervaded by the distilled terror of every tragedy that transpired within it, though usually there is a focal tragedy, a sort of primary trauma.

May Holy Memories Breed Holy Ghosts?

Happy memories breed, of course, happy ghosts. And
holy memories may breed holy ghosts. At any rate, there
are a number of well-authenticated cases of spectral figures associated with holy places.

Trinity Episcopal Cathedral's All Saints Chapel, Trenton, New Jersey, is said to be haunted. Several members
of the cathedral staff, including the Reverend Canon
John A. Van Sant and the Reverend Robert D. White,
told me of happenings such as doors opening and closing
in the chapel, footsteps being heard, and kneelers moving without any visible means of propulsion.

The most recent instance that has come to my attention concerns the old monk at Holy Cross. The monastery
of Holy Cross is in West Park, New York, and Gail
Williams, a parishioner of St. Mary's Episcopal Church in
Keyport, New Jersey, had never been to the monastery
prior to Easter Sunday 1971.

The monastery's Easter service began in the refectory
when the Paschal Candle was lit. From its light, each
monk, at 4:45 A.M., was to take his candle and go to the
chapel to welcome Resurrection morning.

Gail Williams watched as the monks moved up the
aisle. She recognized each one; those she had not formally met, she had seen about the monastery sometime
during her visit. But there was a very old monk whom
she had not seen before. He had great difficulty in getting up from his chair, and she wondered why Brother
William, a monk she knew, didn't help him. She was
annoyed, in fact, that Brother William appeared to avoid
assisting the old monk.

As the cowled figures proceeded up the aisle, the aged
one was last in line—signifying that he had been at the

monastery longest—and the only monk without a lighted candle. Gail Williams wondered at this. She noted his peculiar, almost arthritic gait, and thought, "He really is a very old man."

After the morning Eucharist, Gail Williams, over coffee, asked who the old monk was.

"What old monk?" said Brother Raphael.

She described him, including the great difficulty he had rising from his chair, his shuffling, feeble gait, and the fact that he was last in the procession.

"That sounds like Father Whitall," suggested Brother Raphael.

"I haven't seen him before," Gail Williams said.

"No," replied the monk. "He's dead."

Gail Williams told me this story in a calm, unemotional way, and it was very convincing. When I checked at the monastery with Brother William, he tended to pooh-pooh the incident as having been the result of "suggestion."

"People come here and expect that sort of thing," he said in a kindly, indulgent way. "The ghost idea is a perpetual rumor here. It's kind of fun. The emotional level at Easter is very high."

Brother William's caution in accepting an event as out of the ordinary was understandable, of course, and reflected a pastorally wise prudence. The Church is not primarily concerned, after all, whether an alleged wonderful happening was or was not objectively real, except as that may be relevant to a person's spiritual well-being.

On the other hand, Gail Williams' rector, Canon Pettit, said to me: "There's no question in my mind, from knowing this woman, that she did indeed see a figure and that it was Father Whitall."

The woman had told her rector: "I have always believed in the communion of saints but now even more so."

The deceased monk in question, Edwin Clark Whitall,

was born, interestingly enough, in Woodbury, New Jersey, and baptized in Christ Church. He died at the monastery in 1969, aged ninety years.

The Specter of Liszt

If what Gail Williams saw had objective reality outside her own mind—and I'm inclined to believe it did—was the ghostly figure the spirit form of the dead monk? Or, rather, was it a specific place memory, an image from the past projected on the screen of her mind, sensitized, and made receptive, perhaps, by the high spiritual level of Easter?

Without additional evidence, no one can really say which theory in this case is more plausible. However, there are other cases in which the ghostly presence appears actually to have been that, a presence, and not a mere etheric image. Consider an unusual experience recounted to me by the celebrated organist Virgil Fox.

He was preparing for a recital in old Temple Church, London. Practicing long hours at the church organ, he found himself in the organ loft late one night, alone. He was having problems with the adagio movement in a particularly difficult work by Franz Liszt. He couldn't get it exactly the way he felt it should be.

Pondering the passage, sitting in the vast, darkened church, the only light the one over the organ, Virgil Fox slowly became aware that he was *not* alone. There was, with him, a presence.

The moment the presence obtruded on his awareness, the moment he became conscious of it, however, it receded. When he returned to his music, it returned, lurking in the corners of his mind, subtle but overpoweringly real, the sense of someone benign, wise, and caring.

Then, out of the corner of his eye, the organist saw a

figure. He turned and stared at it directly. It was a smoky form, he said, and it had the face of Liszt.

No words were spoken, either by Virgil Fox or the likeness of the long-dead composer, but, the organist said, it was as though he were being given the understanding of how Liszt wanted that particular passage of his work played. When the figure faded, it left behind a peace, a warmth, a benediction.

It is hard to evaluate such an experience in terms of objective reality, particularly, of course, in the case of a creative genius, with all the imagination that implies.

However, even when full allowance has been made for tricks of perception; wishful thinking; hallucinations, plain or fancy; and other natural explanations, experiences remain that are widespread, well-documented, and, in cumulative terms, irresistibly convincing.

Evidence Too Powerful to Be Denied

In some cases, the evidence of something more than the normal is too powerful to be denied—as in the case of a sad church haunting, a tragic ghost, in which my friends Olga and Ambrose Worrall were involved. Here, surely, more than an etheric image from the past was present; the evidence suggests that an unhappy soul indeed was caught between earth and heaven.

On July 9, 1970, the Worralls (introduced to you in the chapter on healing) were invited by the Reverend Latham Bewley to visit his rectory and church at West Lynn, Kings Lynn, England. The church itself was built in the thirteenth century and is a particularly lovely example of Early English architecture. The rectory, which stands behind the churchyard, dates from a much later period, probably being a mere one hundred and fifty years old. It was in the rectory that Father Bewley in-

troduced the Worralls to his family. He said nothing to
Ambrose or Olga about any psychic disturbance but,
later, he and Ambrose took a stroll in the garden.

What happened is best described in Father Bewley's
own account:

> At the front of the house there is a high lawn
> with two massive cedar trees planted in it. Un-
> der these, Ambrose said he got definite impres-
> sions of worship—pre-christian rites—and of great
> peace. "A good place to meditate," he said.
>
> Then we strolled round the house, past the
> front door towards the former stables, now a
> garage. At the corner of the yard Ambrose
> stopped and said there was a great darkness
> surrounding the garage—it was a place of de-
> pression.
>
> When we approached more closely to the
> building he said he had the definite impression
> that we were drawing near to a "sink-hole."
> He described this to me as a place where ele-
> mental forces re-enter the earth and said that
> one would feel rather depressed in that vicinity.
> He was very definite: The area behind the stable
> had been used for burial, he said, because there
> were a number of earthbound spirits there.
>
> So Olga, who was in the house, was fetched.
> As we walked towards the old stable she stopped
> at the corner of the courtyard and refused to
> go any further. She described it as being very
> dark there. She did go on, at my urging, and
> upon going round the stable immediately said
> that it was an old burial ground and many
> earthbound spirits were there.
>
> On entering the garage Olga became very agi-
> tated and shivered. She put her hands to her
> face and head and almost cried out in despair.

I sensed a great disturbance within her and in the atmosphere, which seemed cold, chilling.

Olga said, in a great torrent of words, that there was a man, a priest there, and that he had taken his life and was bitterly unhappy.

I confirmed this story as true—indeed, had known ever since taking the parish that one of my predecessors had taken his own life there, in the old stable, in very unhappy circumstances. That was in 1940. This knowledge and a sense of urgency about the whole uncanny business had been my main reason for inviting Olga and Ambrose.

I took Olga to the graveside of the priest. His body had been buried in the churchyard, not far from the house and church. It's a simple grave, still tended by a parishioner who always cuts the grass and puts flowers on the grave.

Olga knelt down at the graveside and asked me to pray with her for his peace and for his spirit. This I did readily, having always believed in the power of prayer for both the living and the departed within the Body of Christ.

Olga said a simple, direct prayer for peace and light and for love to surround the priest in his sorrow and despair. She mentioned someone called Eric who was coming to meet the departed priest's spirit, and said that the priest's mother also had welcomed him.

About two weeks later another priest joined me and we said prayers for the departed in the garage, the scene of his tragedy, and behind it, blessed the area and sprinkled it with holy water, and then quietly in the church offered together the Holy Eucharist for the peace of our departed brother in Christ.

After these events, reported Father Bewley, an almost palpable sense of peace descended upon the place where, formerly, torment was felt.

This case represents the type of haunting, in which a spirit, shell-shocked in the battle of life, as it were, is too unhappy, too disoriented, even to realize that death has taken place. Such a soul is said to be "earthbound." There is an associated theory that ghosts that are seen to perform the same, unvarying ritual, time and time again—whether walking the same castle parapet or endlessly re-enacting a murder—are earthbound spirits suffering from "posthumous obsession." Just as a living person in the grip of an obsession may wash his hands incessantly, eternally peer under the bed, or perform any one of a thousand compulsive acts, a confused, unhappy spirit may be driven to perform the same meaningless acts after death.

The therapy of choice is the sort used by Olga Worrall and the priest: loving prayer for the unhappy soul, commending him into the light of God, perhaps asking other kindly spirits to draw near to help. The sacraments of the church have a profound value, since sacramental grace, transcending time and space, also transcends death.

A Priest-Exorcist

A priest-exorcist of note (though he dislikes the word "exorcist" because it implies a militancy that he considers misguided) is my friend the Reverend Canon John Pearce-Higgins, vice chairman of The Churches' Fellowship for Psychical and Spiritual Studies in Britain.

Exorcism, with its implication of expulsion, by force if necessary, is something proper for demons, says Canon Pearce-Higgins, but not for earthbound spirits.

"Such souls," he explains, "are not usually evil, just lost."

In an age of increasing disbelief, said the Canon, there are bound to be more and more people who die and awaken in a state of existence in which they never believed and who, not realizing they are dead, continue to cling to their earthly ways. They are, in a true sense, suspended in limbo, not knowing where to go next in order to further their spiritual life.

"One spirit whom I urged to look for the light said sadly, 'Where *is* the light?'" recalled Pearce-Higgins, "while another said, 'I don't know where to go,' and yet another, 'I am in darkness.'"

In dealing with most hauntings, the Canon, who is Britain's most famous ecclesiastical deghoster, uses a form of requiem service in which the troubled and troubling spirit is bidden to depart in peace. It works.

In some cases, Canon Pearce-Higgins makes use of a spirit medium. His or her function is to go into trance and become an instrument through which the troublesome spirit can communicate and be communicated with. This method seems necessary in chronic cases where the haunting is of very long duration and the symptoms particularly stubborn.

"Clara"

One such recalcitrant spirit came into my life in the summer of 1962. I received an early-morning phone call from Mrs. Betsy Hoffman, who, calmly and matter-of-factly, told me about some very strange things that had been occurring in her house in Philadelphia. She spoke of eerie sounds, odd commotions, and cold spots in the house where the temperature seemed to be subzero while the surrounding area was normal. Could I help?

On this case Bob Lewis and I enlisted the services of the best psychic consultant in the business, Arthur Ford. The three of us arrived at Mrs. Hoffman's address to find a big old house in a very smart section of Philadelphia. Inside, our hostess filled us in on the ghost and its ways.

Repeatedly the sound of "a woman's long skirts whooshing past" was heard. Mysterious bumps occurred in the middle of the night (why this propensity among ghosts for interrupting sleep?). Once, in the upstairs study, the Hoffmans saw a light "flying" around the room near the ceiling; it described "angular configurations," almost like geometric patterns.

When the father, Sterrett Hoffman, became ill and had to go to the hospital, his room was set in order and locked. But in the night, his desk chair was heard scraping across the floor, and the next morning the room was found in disarray—the chair pulled back from the desk, the bedspread crumpled on the floor, books strewn around.

"We straightened up the room and locked it again," said Mrs. Hoffman, "but the same thing happened repeatedly through that summer."

The one responsible for these strange doings, said the Hoffmans, was "Clara." The family had hit on her name by calling out every name they could think of until they found one the ghost responded to by ceasing and desisting from causing a disturbance.

The name Clara made the ghost seem, well, almost motherly. But her pranks, if they were just pranks, could be malicious.

"There was one occasion," said Mrs. Hoffman, "when Janice, the maid, was in the dining room cleaning. I was putting paper in the buffet drawers and had used scissors to cut the paper in the proper shape and had left the scissors on the edge of the buffet.

"Suddenly I heard a crash, turned, and saw the scissors on the floor, and the maid said, 'Mrs. Hoffman, why did you throw the scissors at me?' I said I hadn't thrown them, but she insisted I had.

"Anyway, there were the scissors, lying across the room on the floor, broken in half."

On another occasion, when Mrs. Hoffman was away from the house, she received a phone call from the laundress, who said that the boys' shirts were flying off the railing of the hall banister. The laundress said that as usual she had been ironing in the upstairs sunporch and putting the shirts on the banister to dry. But as soon as she turned around, the shirts all ended up on the floor. And there was no breeze blowing.

When Mrs. Hoffman got home she took over the shirt-ironing but had the same frustrating experience: She put the shirts on the hall railing, then came back a few minutes later to find them on the floor.

"There was only one way to deal with this sort of thing, I'd found," said Mrs. Hoffman. "I yelled, 'Clara! Clara! Will you leave these shirts alone!' That was the end of that episode. You have to get tough with her."

Shortly after we arrived at the Hoffman house, Arthur Ford excused himself and went upstairs to use the lavatory. He came back in a few minutes looking as if he had seen a ghost. He sat down, adjusted his cigar in his mouth, and said in a matter-of-fact voice: "I just met Clara in the upstairs hall."

Ford went on to describe her as "a seemingly old lady with the long skirt, prim, high neckline, and the little cap they used to wear in those times"—a description that fit that given independently by several people who had seen the ghost.

The medium said the ghost kept waving her arm, pointing out the upstairs hall window. He asked the Hoffmans if there was water somewhere behind the house.

Mrs. Hoffman confirmed that there was a pool, but Arthur said no, it wasn't a pool; some larger body of water—a pond or lake.

"I saw her in the water in her clothes," Ford said, "being sucked down. She drowned. That's why she's around. You'll have to help Clara."

Ford's information gave the Hoffmans some clues to work on. Their first step was to try to find Clara's full name, and, by checking newspaper morgues, the local historical society, and old deeds, they did find it: Clara Johnson.

Later, a pretty full history of old Clara was elaborated in a Parastudy Group Report by Betty Spickler (*Parastudy Report*, Chester Heights, Pa. [May 1963]).

Can a Spirit Be Released?

A psychic, Mrs. Regina Lake, described the spinster Clara as having lived in the house with her niece, whom she had raised, and a "dark-skinned handyman, probably an Indian," who did the work around the place. Even at best, said the medium, Clara was antisocial, and as she got older she became more suspicious of people and more domineering toward her niece who, largely because of Clara's objections, never married.

After a fall downstairs, the old woman's eccentric ways became still more pronounced. The medium said Clara developed what was probably a tumor on the brain, and slowly became insane. In her last days she wandered the house incessantly.

A woman relative who came to help take care of Clara was the victim who drowned, not Clara herself, said this medium. Standing by the pond behind the house, the relative took a dizzy spell and fell into the deep water. The only one at home to hear her cries was old Clara, rocking away in her chair, deep in the darkness of insanity.

Another who visited the Hoffman house to make Clara's acquaintance and to seek to "release" her was the great Irish medium, Eileen Garrett, who, in the heydey of her mediumship, helped deghost many places.

Going into trance, Mrs. Garrett described the unhappy spirit, verifying much of what other mediums had told the Hoffmans. At one point, the medium, still in trance, got to her feet and walked into the yard behind the house. Fearing she might fall, Mrs. Hoffman tried to restrain her, but the entranced medium, pushing away the hand, said impatiently: "I am following the path."

This struck the Hoffmans as very evidential: When first they moved into the house they had removed a brick path from the yard, and it was this path, now totally overgrown, that Mrs. Garrett, in her strange psychic thrall, was following.

Eileen Garrett gave the Hoffmans instructions on how to deal with their unbidden guest so as to "release" her—instructions that are applicable to other such cases.

It was vital to have a "right attitude" toward the ghostly visitor, said the medium, to think of her in love and concern and with a desire to assist her. It was helpful, the medium added, to express these feelings in thoughts and meditations, as well as aloud in prayer. Speak to the ghost when its presence is felt, she advised, knowing that if it is a true spirit, and not merely an etheric image, it will hear and possibly respond.

Carrying out these suggestions, the Hoffmans noticed that Clara's visitations became fewer and briefer. Then, in February 1965, Arthur Ford gave the Hoffmans a trance sitting in his Philadelphia apartment.

"Clara is gone and will not be there ever again," Fletcher said.

Later, in January 1972, Mrs. Hoffman, when I asked

her if they had heard of Clara again, said: "Not since Fletcher told us she had left."

As hauntings go, the Clara case is a sort of hybrid, partway between the classic type haunting and the poltergeist. In the classic type, the manifestations are confined almost entirely to sights and sounds, and, occasionally, smells. People see apparitions, hear weird noises, smell strange or incongruous odors. By contrast, in the typical poltergeist haunting, the manifestations are limited to physical phenomena: Objects move, doors open and shut, plaster splits, beds shake or even levitate. There may also be characteristic eerie sounds, most often scratchings, raps, and thumps, or what are described as "sawing" noises.

The word poltergeist, from the German, means literally "noisy spirit," or, as sometimes given, "mischievous" spirit. But poltergeist hauntings may reveal malice as well as mere mischief. In dealing with such troublesome cases, again parapsychology has much to teach theology.

The Adolescent Theory of Poltergeists

One eerie poltergeist mystery involved Bob Lewis and me, and another pastoral colleague, the Reverend Roy Grace, in a psychic detective story. Unable to track the mystery to its lair, we were able to shed enough light on it that the sinister manifestations ceased.

Dr. Grace, who is a Presbyterian minister in Philadelphia and a deep student of psychic research, received a call for help from a photographer whose studio was not far from the pastor's church. The man was obviously unnerved. He said that very strange events were going on in his studio that threatened to ruin his business and possibly his sanity.

The man's color portraits, which were outstanding, had

earned him a prized reputation in photographic circles and led to his becoming the official photographer for a number of large high schools in the Philadelphia area. These accounts formed a major part of his income. Now, he said, he was in grave danger of losing them. The problem was a plague of inexplicable scratches, which appeared across the face in many of the high school portraits. The scratches appeared on both the finished photos and the proofs, despite the fact that the photographer processed and mounted most of these himself. In nearly every case, the scratch disfigured the eyes of the subject.

At a loss for any technical explanation of the scratches, the photographer started taking work home with him, processing the student portraits there and carrying them back to the studio the next day. However, when he removed the photos from the envelopes the following morning, he found, more often than not, the same scratches across the subjects' eyes.

The scratches varied somewhat in length and position but always looked as though they had been gouged out by fingernails. However, it seemed impossible to the photographer that anybody could have tampered with the last batch of portraits, which he had processed and sealed in envelopes himself.

Soon after this, the curse of the scratches spread to the negatives as well. Many of the students had to be rephotographed. Then, like some insidious infection, the scratches began appearing on large, prize color portraits —of brides, children, and other subjects—which hung on the walls of the studio.

Desperate, torn between the fear of being thought mad and the greater fear of being ruined, the photographer called the police. When he told them his story they said, quite bluntly, that it sounded like a publicity stunt and declined to investigate.

Eastman Kodak was contacted and sent a team of

experts to check on the bizarre epidemic of scratches that disfigured only portraits, and, then, only the eyes.

The experts found nothing to explain the mystery. But one of the inspectors left his briefcase on a table in the photographer's studio, in plain sight of everybody, and when he picked it up later, there were the familiar, deep scratches in the leather.

Dr. Grace, being familiar with poltergeist cases and what parapsychology has discovered about them, asked the inevitable first question: "Do you have an adolescent or young person working for you?"

"Yes," said the photographer. "At least, she's a woman about twenty. And now that you mention it, these things usually happen when she's here.

"But I can swear that the marks are on the photos when she opens the envelopes. She opens them in front of the students, to show them the pictures when they come into the studio. I'm the one who puts those pictures in the envelopes. And the envelopes show no sign of having been tampered with."

Dr. Grace's question did not imply that the young person employed in the studio was causing the scratches deliberately. Hoaxing, however, is a possibility to be kept in mind. In some poltergeist cases the agent has proved to be a flesh-blood prankster, the antics having been performed either consciously, or unconsciously while the prankster was in a mildly abnormal mental state.

But the common role of an adolescent as "focal person" in poltergeist hauntings is more complex than the mere question of possible fraud. Some psychic researchers favor the theory that the poltergeist is not a disembodied spirit but a split-off portion of the focal person's unconscious mind. It is as though the adolescent, through some emotional shock, has suffered, in the words of Nandor Fodor, a "psychic lobotomy" that caused part of his mind to float free and function more or less autonomously, on its own. It is this free-floating bundle of raw psychic energy that propels objects through the air, smashes crockery, causes raps and thumps—or puts scratches on photographs.

After talking with the photographer, Roy Grace phoned Arthur Ford. The medium immediately asked the same question: "Is there a young person working there?" Told of the young woman, Ford's advice was terse: "Get rid of her." That, he said, would stop the epidemic of scratches.

Dr. Grace contacted me about the case and, without knowing what the others had asked, I put the same question about an adolescent around the place. The description of the case, its eerie, rather menacing overtones ("I'll scratch your eyes out"), aroused my pastoral concern, and Bob Lewis and I met Dr. Grace at the studio to pursue the mystery.

We were introduced to the photographer and his wife, and to the young woman who served as his assistant. In conversation, which I kept deliberately casual, the young woman struck me as a somewhat moody person but not at all unpleasant.

The photographer and his wife, who liked the girl, were reluctant to believe that she could have anything to do with the bizarre scratches, even unconsciously, and they refused to consider firing her. Dr. Grace offered a compromise suggestion: Give her a two-week leave of absence to see if the scratches continued or ceased.

While the photographer was pondering this suggestion, the young woman got wind of what was going on, that she was, in some vague way, under suspicion in the matter of the mysterious scratches, and promptly quit her job and went to work for a bank. So far as we know, the bank was not troubled by the poltergeist—but neither was the photographer. With the girl's departure, the scratches, too, ceased to appear.

Weighing the evidence, I wondered if there weren't still a missing piece to the puzzle. Granted, a person, usually an adolescent, can generate, quite unconsciously, a psychic force that produces poltergeist phenomena; isn't it possible that, at the same time, the young person's biological energies may be used by some outside agency? In other words, could the poltergeist person be an unwitting medium who provides the psychic energy by which a spirit can vent its malice?

It appears to be a rule that discarnate spirits can manifest in physical actions only by siphoning the necessary psychic power from a living person. I asked the photographer if there were anyone, living or departed, who disliked him, or with whom he was in great conflict, either about his work or his personal life.

"There's only one person who would appreciate what's happened here," said the photographer after a moment's thought. "My father."

He explained: "He had this business before me and was jealous of me. He resented my talent. We disagreed very much for years and were at odds. He couldn't accept my ability."

Was it, then, a case of the deceased father, still holding his fierce resentment of his son, suddenly able to express it because of the presence of the unconsciously mediumistic young woman?

If this were the case, the father, though at that moment he might still harbor the resentment, deprived of his unwitting medium, would not be able to vent it.

Automatic Writing

We could not tie up all the loose ends of the mystery, but the photographer was delivered from his plague of scratches. And a little later, some curious information came to light that tended to corroborate my suspicions in the case.

Dr. Grace uses hypnosis in the context of pastoral counseling, and one of his subjects, a young man, developed an unusual facility at automatic writing—script produced without the aid of the conscious mind. The pastor, when the young man was in a deep trance, asked him about the poltergeist case, without giving any details, and suggested that answers might come to him later through automatic writing.

What followed was extraordinary. Much later, at home, the young man felt prompted to pick up his pen and to let it write on its own, as it seemed; the script took the form of a communication in which a declared though unidentified spirit claimed responsibility for trying to "hurt" another for "revenge." The alleged communicator said he had been dead many years and the reason he had not tormented his victim sooner was that he had lacked "a proper channel or instrument."

Since this young man knew nothing of the nature of the case we had been investigating, the content of the automatic script struck us as peculiarly apt and suggestive.

The mature Christian viewpoint toward hauntings is that, though natural causes for such phenomena always should be sought first, genuine cases do occur. These are of different sorts, some appearing to be the playback of images from the past, others the discharge of raw psychic energy from the unconscious mind of a living person, and still others the actions of discarnate spirits.

In the case of a discarnate spirit, the Christian approach is to seek to help and heal the disoriented, earthbound soul who has lost the light and needs to find his way again. The means of helping are the same as those for helping someone in a similar plight on this side of the veil: prayer, the sacraments, the grace of our Lord Jesus Christ.

7

MEDIUMSHIP
Do the Dead Communicate?

The most controversial question in psychic research no doubt is this one: *Do the dead communicate?*

Some psychic researchers, as skeptical as the next man about human survival after death (the notion that all parapsychologists want to prove an afterlife is quite mistaken), object that this question begs the point by assuming the very thing to be proved, namely, that the dead are in a position to communicate.

The question of whether the dead *do* communicate, is based on the assumption that they *can* communicate. And about this little matter there is, among psychic researchers, as among many others, considerable disagreement.

However, whether the dead communicate is a valid question and can be easily rephrased to overcome the objection that it assumes too much. Put it this way: *Are there messages, said to emanate from the dead, which, on grounds of logic and reason, seem most likely to come from that source?*

C. J. Ducasse, a distinguished philosopher of psychic research, said the problem boiled down to this: If a friend of yours, John Doe, is reported missing and presumed dead in a plane crash, though no body was found, and six months later you receive a telephone call purporting to be from him, how can you know whether it is he on the line?

One way would be by the sound of his voice. But suppose, because of a poor telephone connection, he could make himself heard only to the operator, who, therefore, served as go-between in your conversation. Under these circumstances, how would you go about determining if it were your friend on the other end of the line?

You would put questions, surely, to which your friend, and possibly only he and you, knew the answers: Who was our teacher when we were in Grade Seven together? Who caught us smoking in the back shed that time? What was the amount of the loan you gave me once that I never paid back? These sorts of questions.

If the caller, communicating through the operator, gave correct answers to such questions, and cited other evidential details that your friend Joe would know, you well might conclude that the reports were wrong, that your friend was not dead but alive and talking with you at that moment.

This is analogous to the situation in a successful sitting with a medium. Messages come, in the medium's voice, as a rule, and sometimes in his language, but conveying information that seems most plausibly to originate with some deceased friend who indeed claims to be communicating.

Evidence

Consider some evidential cases from my investigations of mediums.

Considering my friendship with Arthur Ford, the mediumistic virtuoso of our time, it is not surprising that my best survival evidence has come through him. Once, when Ford was in trance, Fletcher, his spirit guide or trance personality, spoke of Mr. and Mrs. William Miller, who were communicants of my parish.

"Robert Miller is here and he is glad to meet you," said Fletcher. "You know his mother."

This was a son of the Millers who had died in his twenties of cancer; I hadn't known him, but his parents had spoken of him to me.

"Tell his mother that he lives," Fletcher continued. "Tell her that he loves her, and tell her especially not to worry. She worries too much. Tell her that a strange man came to tell you these things. She thinks she saw him once, but they didn't believe her. Tell her that she did see him, that she wasn't dreaming.

"Robert says that sometimes she picks up his picture and brings it to her face. I can almost superimpose myself on the picture, he says, and smile at her."

Then the entranced medium winced, and his hand went to his leg.

"My leg hurts," he muttered. "Trouble there."

Mrs. Miller, I knew, always had wondered what led to her son's fatal illness. Now the entranced medium was saying: "Tell her cancer started when a baseball hit him in the leg."

"But Fletcher," I demurred, "suppose she gets upset emotionally when I tell her this."

"You will know what to say," he murmured.

Well, apparently I did know what to say, because Mrs. Miller accepted the message gratefully, acknowledging that it was correct in every particular.

The question, of course, is: Where did Ford get the information? He said he got it from the surviving mind of the deceased boy.

One objection commonly made to mediumistic messages is why are they so trivial. One answer is that they are not all trivial (I'll be sharing with you some decidedly untrivial messages in this book). But, on the other hand, isn't the bit of evidence that is likely to be most convincing also likely to be the most trivial, the most insignificant? Many people may have known that the boy in the previous incident had died of cancer, but who, except his mother, would have known that she often lifted his photograph to her lips? Or that the cause of the fatal malignant growth was his having been struck by a baseball? Were these messages really trivial?

In another incident, the evidential remark was in one sense trivial, I suppose, yet all the more striking to me. During a sitting with Ford, a communicator identified herself as a woman I had buried just a day or so before, and admonished: "You could at least have said a few nice words about me."

I was chagrined—as chagrined as though the deceased were sitting there in the room talking to me (as indeed at that moment she seemed to be). You see, the funeral, a very small one, came at a time when I was hard-pressed by pastoral duties, and I had omitted any eulogy of the deceased. The medium could not have known this, but here, through Fletcher, I was being gently reproached.

(A fellow priest, when I told him this story, said: "You have more damn trouble with the dead than I do with the living!")

Arthur Ford often presented convincing messages from the dead during his platform clairvoyance before large audiences, as well as in the privacy of the séance room. At such times he was not in a trance but in what he described as "a sort of half-hypnotized state" in which he could "hear" the thoughts of the dead.

My friend Henry L. Marzell, a prominent real-estate broker in Clifton, New Jersey, told me how he attended an Arthur Ford lecture in Clifton, New Jersey, in the late 1950s.

"It was the first time I'd ever seen Ford," said Mr. Marzell. "There were at least five hundred people in the audience. Ford couldn't have known I was going to be at that lecture even if he had known me, which he didn't.

"Anyway, he pointed in my direction, then singled me out of the five hundred in that auditorium, and said, 'There's a man who comes to you. I see him in a sort of policeman's uniform, or a uniform worn in a court. Something like that.'

"This had great meaning to me. My father was a sergeant-at-arms in a courtroom. I knew immediately that it was my father Ford was describing, and I believe that he was there, communicating."

Sometimes the most unlikely people popped in at Ford's séances. Once a message came to me from a man who said he knew me but I didn't know him. His name was Stoerrle, Ernest Stoerrle, he said, and he had seen me in Woodbury!

Inquiring in town about him, I found that he was the deceased owner of a small hotel in Woodbury, some two blocks from Christ Church. The interesting, and significant, sequel is that when I mentioned the incident to one of my parishioners she, a good friend of Mrs. Stoerrle, the man's widow, passed on the story to her. To Mrs. Stoerrle it was "amazing": She and her husband had talked many times about the possibility of life after death and this, she believed, was a sign to her from him.

If, as some skeptics might suggest, it may have been telepathy on the medium's part—that is, the facts about Mr. Stoerrle were picked from my mind by the medium's ESP—I point out that this (besides being in itself a good trick) seems unlikely, since to my knowledge I wasn't even aware what the deceased looked like. He certainly was not in my thoughts at that séance. Where, then, did the message come from if not from the mind of the dead but still living Mr. Stoerrle?

Bits and Pieces of Information to Be Explained Away

Sometimes Fletcher-Ford (it was hard to separate the
two in my mind, in one sense; yet, in another, they were
utterly different) gave information that apparently wasn't
known to anyone living but was confirmed by investigation. Thus a woman had a sitting with Ford in which her
deceased husband urged her to see a doctor as soon as
possible.

"I don't want to frighten you," said the communicator, "but you should be medically examined because I
can see a gray area. You have a malignancy, and it must
be checked immediately."

The woman went to a doctor who, as one might imagine, listened with some skepticism (properly, no doubt)
to the story of her dead husband's diagnosis. A medical
examination revealed no serious problems, the doctor
said.

Soon after, however, X-rays detected a cancer that
medical treatment was unable to arrest. It seems likely
that the malignancy was present, in an incipient form,
when the warning came through Ford.

In a sitting with Arthur Ford, Canon Gerald Minchin,
then of St. Mary's Parish, Haddon Heights, New Jersey,
took along his wife, whom the medium expected, and a
cousin, whom the medium didn't expect. Significantly,
it was the cousin, Mrs. Ethel Long, who got the most
evidential messages that day (weakening considerably
the theory of some skeptics that mediums are successful
only with sitters on whom they have had a chance to do
prior research).

Ford told Mrs. Long, whom he had never met, of
course, that her husband had died nine years before, that

his name was Ray, and that his work had been carried on
"underground" in some way.

This was correct. Her husband Ray, dead nine years,
had been a mining engineer.

Significantly, Ford correctly divined that Mrs. Long
was suffering from a growth, but assured her that she
would have many years of moderately good health, a
prediction that was still valid ten years later as she continued to live a productive life.

However, to return to the matter of trivial matters as
convincing evidence of communication from the dead:
The remark of Ford's that most struck Mrs. Long was a
totally facetious allusion to her having become a religious
bargain-hunter.

"You've always been the religious one, Ethel," her deceased husband said, "and now you're shopping around
for a different church."

Mrs. Long acknowledged that at the time, contrary to
her custom, she was attending services at different
churches.

Also trivial, if you like, but nonetheless striking to
Canon Minchin, was a remark said to come from his
father, dead for thirty-five years.

"Your father had white, curly hair," said Ford, "and he
says they called him Curly."

Canon Minchin chuckled. Who but his dad, he thought,
could have come up with that nickname? Who, indeed?
And that, of course, was the point of it.

Oh, I know, better than most people, I assure you, that
mediumistic espionage exists, that some so-called mediums keep files on prospective sitters. There is evidence
that even genuine mediums such as Ford, sometimes,
through moral weakness and human frailty, fall into this
despicable trick. But even allowing for fraud, there are
too many examples of what Ford used to call "tremendous
trivia"—these odd, obscure bits and pieces of information
—for all to be explained away. And some of them seem

to have come from the minds of dead persons, since no other source, to me at least, appears conceivable.

Take the matter of names. Are names trivia? In one sense they are; shouldn't the dead spend their time doing something more than reporting their own names? This is a typical objection from a certain sort of skeptic. On the other hand, if a purported spirit communicator *doesn't* know his own name, or a pet nickname his mother used when he was a child, something seems wrong.

Arthur Ford was, in a mediumistic sense, a great name-dropper. I've known a Ford sitting to yield as many as thirty names of individuals, both discarnate and incarnate, often woven into a meaningful and complex pattern.

In a sitting with my mother, the medium told her: "Your mother was a Bohemian, a Polack or something." He then mentioned the name "Levitsky," and said it wasn't just right but the best he could do.

Well, it was quite good enough to be astonishing. My maternal grandmother was a Bohemian, and her maiden name was Richetsky. Ford, or Fletcher, was very close. And I can attest that there was no conceivable way (conceivable to my mother or to me, at any rate) that Ford could have ferreted out these facts. If this information, garbled slightly though it was, did not come from my deceased grandmother, where did it come from?

On another occasion, speaking of tremendous trivia and names, Ford was describing clairvoyantly a church in Scranton, Pennsylvania, that he had never seen (and doing it quite accurately) when, apropos of nothing, he said: "Some of the furniture belonged to Dudley Stark's father. He keeps talking about 'Lord save us.'"

We had no idea what Fletcher was talking about. The Right Reverend Dudley Stark, we knew, was at the time Episcopal Bishop of Rochester, New York, but what did his father's furniture have to do with anything, particularly a church in Scranton?

On checking, we found that Bishop Stark's father, then

deceased, had lived in Scranton, where he ran a furniture business. And, yes, he once had sold some furniture to the church in question. The church secretary later affirmed that his friends often called him "Lord save us," a phrase he frequently used.

Are Medium Messages Trivial?

Trivial? Yes. Convincing evidence of communication from the dead? Yes—to me. And to many others who sat with Ford.

A Presbyterian minister, the Reverend Roy Grace, had many examples of Ford's tremendous trivia. Once, a communicator in a séance said she was Gladys Goodfellow and had met Dr. Grace in, of all places, Addis Ababa, in 1950.

"I had no recollection of any such person," Dr. Grace said, "but she went on to mention that her husband was in Ethopia at the time as an economic adviser to Haile Selassie, that she had returned to the States and died here.

"I checked these facts out completely and found the woman was in Addis Ababa during a visit I made as a mission board officer and that though I had no memory of meeting her, she had heard me preach at the Swedish Church there."

On another occasion Dr. Grace was told by Fletcher that he had an ancestor, described as a "Dr. Harvey," who lived in Philadelphia a century ago and used minerals and herbs in his work.

"I do have such an ancestor," said Roy Grace, "though Ford had no knowledge from me about him, and he did work as Fletcher described. I might say, too, that he wasn't at all in my mind when Fletcher gave me that message."

In the trance state, Arthur Ford's mind seemed unchained from his body so that he was able to project it to a distance and bring back information. Once Fletcher took an "astral trip" to look in on my mother, about whom I had asked. (My mother lived some distance from me then, and we had not communicated for a little time.)

"Your mother's had a fall," Fletcher said after a long pause, speaking in a strained, breathy way (almost as if he were out of breath from his trip). "She slipped or something. But her condition is . . ." And then he went on to describe her physical condition.

When I phoned my mother I found that she had fallen that day, and her condition, which wasn't serious, corresponded exactly to what Fletcher had told me.

"Cross-Correspondence"

What can be particularly convincing as evidence for communication from discarnate minds is the complex patterning called "cross-correspondences." This term, and there have been some impressive and famous cases, refers to the phenomenon in which independent messages through different mediums fit together, like the pieces of a jigsaw puzzle, to form a meaningful pattern. Such a pattern seems to preclude the possibility of even super ESP as the explanation. The only hypothesis that appears adequate is that different discarnate minds, communicating through different mediums, wove the pattern.

Consider a significant case. It involved Bob Lewis as much as me, and, in addition to Arthur Ford's, the mediumship of Olga and Ambrose Worrall. Besides providing evidence of cross-correspondences, the case offers an insight into how and why events sometimes happen as they do, and whether coincidence is always simply that or something more.

It started at a sitting with the Worralls. It was this couple's lovely custom to observe every night at nine o'clock a "quiet time" of meditation and stillness before God, and on this particular evening Bob Lewis and I were there, along with another friend, Clement Tamburrino. The date, which is significant to the story, was August 24, 1968.

As at other quiet times we had attended, this one was mainly for healing prayer and meditation on behalf of those in need. At one point, however, Olga said to Canon Lewis: "Bob, there's a Father John present. He's standing right by you. I can see him. Do you know a Father John?"

"Yes, Olga," replied Lewis, "that has meaning for me." (The idea is to be direct in responses to a medium but not to give more information than necessary.)

The Father John known to Bob Lewis was the late vicar of All Saints Church in Hershey, Pennsylvania, the Reverend John Treater, who had developed a sort of posthumous friendship with Lewis—posthumous because Treater died in a car crash, and he and Lewis had never met. However, in an Arthur Ford sitting, Father Treater had communicated with Bob Lewis and said that he wanted to guide and help him all he could in his work in the priesthood. Lewis accepted the offer of discarnate friendship with gratitude.

Anyway, now Olga Worrall was saying: "This man is working with you and will help you. He says, 'You don't have a church of your own,' or at any rate you're not in charge. But you're going to have your own church very soon."

A curious coincidence: Unknown to the Worralls, the priest as whose associate Bob Lewis was then working, Canon Gerald Minchin, only four days before had come to Lewis and told him in confidence that he planned to retire in December. Canon Minchin had not told even the bishop of his plans; Bob Lewis was the only one to know. Now, through the lips of a medium, came a message about the prospect of a church of his own.

"They're placing a church right down over your head," Olga Worrall continued. "Oh, my, it's as if they were crowning you with it."

After the sitting, Lewis and Clem Tamburrino and I agreed among ourselves not to mention this matter to anybody.

The next event in the chain—or, at least, it seemed to me that a chain was developing—was when, a few days later, the senior warden of St. Mary's Church, Haddon Heights, where Bob Lewis was curate, pledged his support to Lewis as Canon Minchin's successor as rector.

Curious about whether there was indeed a chain of events being forged, I asked Arthur Ford for a sitting, mentioning nothing of what had happened. That sitting, which Bob Lewis and I attended, was on September 17 (about three weeks after the sitting with the Worralls).

There was the usual ritual of blindfolding himself, breathing deeply and rhythmically for three or four minutes, with loud sighs and exhalations, and then Ford passed into the trance state. His head, which had dropped forward on his chest, rose, and the familiar voice of Fletcher spoke.

"Several people are here," he said. "One man I have not seen before, Duncan. He says he is happy to be here. Somebody says you are causing quite a bit of excitement and speculation."

These remarks were directed at Lewis, who had served as curate under the Reverend James M. Duncan when in Washington, D.C., and later had taken part in his funeral. Duncan, we knew, was the sort of man who would have been interested in Bob Lewis becoming rector anyway, and the sort of man who would have pushed his way through a crowd to speak to him. One could almost imagine him saying to other would-be communicators there: "Make way, I want to reach Father Lewis."

Fletcher said, speaking for Duncan, that there was

going to be a big change for one of us, but it wasn't me, because he didn't see me leaving my parish.

He told Bob Lewis that he would stay where he was but on "a different level."

Through Fletcher, the deceased Father Duncan then asked: "Did the bishop O.K. it?"

There was a pause, then Fletcher said that the vestry certainly approved of Lewis as rector and the bishop would too.

"I greet the rector," Fletcher said, as though the matter were settled.

"There is a lady here," he told Bob, "who says she is your grandmother, and she is wiping her eyes—making a gesture of weeping—but they are the kind of tears a woman has when she is happy."

Bob Lewis and I were impressed by this sitting because we felt certain Ford could not have known of Canon Minchin's plan to retire and the fact that there was, therefore, an opening for a rector at St. Mary's. The information seemed peculiarly evidential as independent confirmation of what Olga Worrall had said. But the final test of the matter, we knew, would be what happened at St. Mary's.

What happened was that the Reverend Robert J. Lewis, after a unanimous vote of the vestry and the bishop's approval, became rector of St. Mary's. In the Episcopal Church it was unusual enough for a curate to step into such a key position, but to happen with advance information from the other side, through not one but two mediums—well, nothing quite like it, I'm sure, had happened before in the Church.

A Sitting with Bishop Pike's Medium

In this case, the mediumistic communications, from any standpoint, were hardly trivial. Nor were other messages

I've received, such as one with considerable moral and spiritual portent that came through the noted British medium Ena Twigg.

When I first sat with Mrs. Twigg in her modest London home, it was before she had made the front pages as one of Bishop Pike's mediums. That came later, after the bishop, distressed by poltergeist phenomena in his Cambridge apartment following the death of his son, sought out Mrs. Twigg. Pike, dressed in ordinary street clothes, came with a friend of the medium, the Reverend Canon John Pearce-Higgins.

In the séance, with Pike offering no clue to his identity, Ena Twigg immediately seemed to tune in on the dead son's thoughts.

"I failed the test," she said, trying to interpret for a spirit communicator whom she described as a confused and unhappy young man. "I tried to get your attention by moving things."

Pike took these to be references to his son's suicide while under the influence of drugs and to the mysterious movement of objects in Pike's apartment, which had prompted the visit to the medium. Further communications came at that sitting, which the bishop accepted as genuine contacts with his son.

In my first sitting with Mrs. Twigg, the results were wholly convincing, though less spectacular, no doubt, than Bishop Pike's, since my circumstances were less spectacular. However, the communicator at my sitting, as at Pike's, was somebody who felt he had "failed the test" and who was eager to let me know that so far as he could he was trying to set things right.

"I smell alcohol," the medium said to me. "Did you have someone close to you in the family who was a heavy drinker? He's saying that he has to make amends because he has been unhappy in the next world. In this world he built a cage for himself and now he's still trying to free himself from it."

There were plenty of evidential details: The man had a good brain, she said, but became neurotic, and this was why he drank. There were three people on earth who still felt sad about the effect he had had on their lives, she noted, adding: "He sends his love to Lillian and asks you to do what you can to set things right."

All this fit my Uncle Bob, who had been an alcoholic, had severe emotional problems in addition to his drinking, though he was highly intelligent, and had caused particular heartache to his sister and her two daughters with whom he lived. One of the daughters was named Lillian.

No trivia here but an agonized cry for forgiveness and redemption from someone who had learned late, though not too late, that death does not end our spiritual problems but merely postpones them.

A Housewife Becomes a Noted Musician . . . with a Little Help from a Friend

It's an ironic coincidence that a few years ago in Britain a savage critic of Spiritualism (I'm critical of some aspects of Spiritualism but not, I trust, savagely so) demanded why, if communication with the dead was real, only the nobodies of the astral world, as he put it, seemed to communicate. Where were Beethoven and Bach? he wanted to know. Surely one new Beethoven sonata would do more to accredit communication with the dead than a thousand messages from dear old Aunt Suzy!

The ironic coincidence to which I referred was that shortly after this blast, a British medium claimed to be receiving music from, of all people, Beethoven and Bach, as well as such lesser lights as Liszt, Chopin, Schubert, Debussy, and Rachmaninoff. Incredibly, the lady's music was good enough to induce some of Britain's leading musicologists at least to take a second look at her claims.

The lady in question was Rosemary Brown, a middle-aged London housewife with no credentials whatever for becoming a musical medium. One might think that somebody picked to convey music from the titans on the other side should have at least a modicum of talent, just to get things started. Mrs. Brown had none. Mary Firth, a music expert who tested her, said that Rosemary Brown was even *below* average in natural musical ability. Yet she produced, and is still producing, a stream of compositions of sufficiently high quality to impress the critics.

Humphrey Searle, Britain's leading Liszt expert, examined a piece called "Grübelei" (Pondering), which Mrs. Brown said came from the master himself, and pronounced it authentically, uncanny, in Liszt's style. Richard Rodney Bennett, a noted composer, paid Rosemary Brown what is probably the supreme compliment from one musician to another: "Some of the Beethoven is so good I couldn't have faked it myself."

Not all the critics raved about Mrs. Brown's music. Some raved against it, largely on the grounds that her pieces were "second-rate rewrites" of lesser-known works of the masters. However, even second-rate rewrites, if that were all, would be astonishing from a woman who seven or eight years ago, when the music started coming, could play hardly a note on the piano. (Today her playing has improved considerably due, she says, to tutelage from Rachmaninoff, who of course has been dead for some thirty years.)

Mrs. Brown's music is good enough to have been presented on two Philips recordings, performed on the British Broadcasting Corporation's radio and television programs, published by Novello & Company, Ltd., and played by such piano artists as Louis Kentner and Hepzibah Menuhin. Not bad for a housewife from London's distinctly unfashionable East End.

Much of Mrs. Brown's music has a religious cast. She says that Liszt, who apparently liked to live it up on earth, has become very devout and often speaks of Christ. Mrs. Brown's favorite piece, which she played at a recital in London's Southwark Cathedral, is Liszt's "Jesus Walking on the Water."

Not being a professional musician, I have no competence to make a technical judgment on Rosemary Brown's work. However, at least one musicologist, Professor Ian Parrott, who teaches at Aberystwyth College, Wales, says he believes her music does come from the astral spheres, or wherever it is exactly that Beethoven, Bach, and company are still composing. A member of the Society for Psychical Research, Professor Parrott, whom I met with Mrs. Brown, is uniquely qualified to judge her as a musician and as a medium. He scores her high on both counts.

"Admittedly," he said to me, "some of her music is not as good as the rest of her work. But many critics treat it rather like an inferior music student's exercise. They don't have any concept of the psychic side at all, and if you haven't got that, it's very hard to judge.

"If there are imperfections in the music they are not the imperfections of any mature student I know. They are something quite different—some breakdown in communication, if you like.

"There is no reason to suggest that it isn't genuine Liszt at one end coming through Rosemary at this end and perhaps not always coming through perfectly. There may be something wrong but, I repeat, not because it's inferior music or an inferior composer at all. It's a breakdown in communication, a problem in the art of mediumship.

"In spite of the communication problem, however, some

of the compositions are superb, such as the piece called 'Grübelei' by Liszt. It's one that he might well have written in his lifetime. I hope he gets more music to us through Rosemary."

Obviously, for Professor Parrott there is no doubt that Rosemary Brown's music comes from a source outside herself.

Talking to her, it's hard not to believe that. Mrs. Brown, for all her transparent honesty and natural goodness, does not sound like the sort of person who could produce the sort of music she does.

She's merely a stenographer, she says, and the music is "given" to her—sometimes by her hands being guided over the piano keys ("as though the spirit composer had put on my hands like gloves," she describes it); sometimes by her hand being guided to write down the notes; but usually by the music being simply "dictated" to her. A session with one of her dead composers, as she recounts it, sounds very much as though he were there in the flesh giving her a music lesson.

More than her music has a religious flavor, I discovered, for Rosemary Brown's mediumship is leavened by a deep faith in God and a sense of being linked to Christ.

"I view this whole thing as a spiritual rather than a musical breakthrough," she told me. "I feel the composers are using me to prove to the world once and for all that life goes on after death; they are doing this by proving their own continued existence. They hope to prove it by creating music in their distinctive styles that I certainly couldn't write.

"The composers want to pour forth a spiritual blessing to mankind, to attune us all to more God-consciousness."

Rosemary Brown said that before a composing session, to clear her mind for "receiving," she prepares by meditation.

"And I always meditate upon God and Christ," she said, "because I believe that God manifested through Christ. That is the basis of my thinking. In that sense, I'm bound up very much with the Christian attitude."

What Is the Next World Like?

Mediumistic trivia? Rosemary Brown's music can't be called that. Listen sometime, if you haven't already, to her Liszt-inspired composition "Jesus Walking on the Water," and as its silvery beauty washes over you, ponder the mystery of a humble, untutored woman who yielded as a spiritual channel to something, or Someone, as I believe, higher than herself.

Besides messages evidential of the fact of survival, others are important in shedding light on the important issue: the *how* of survival.

If the dead live on, where? What is the next world like? For a Christian, it's significant to know whether mediumistic descriptions accord with the Church's teaching on the afterlife. Are heaven and hell part of it? And if so, where, and what, are they—places, states of mind; eternal, temporary?

In my psychic explorations, descriptions of dying and the afterdeath experience that I accept as authentic have come through mediums.

What do discarnate communicators tell about the experience of dying? What is it like to die?

Fletcher once said that dying is easier, less traumatic, for those who know what to expect because "they don't have to shed a lot of false beliefs, which can take time, you know, even over here."

Dying, he said, is rather like falling asleep. The awakening may come sooner or later, depending on the individual's state of enlightenment.

"Sometimes, when people come over," said Fletcher,

"we have to put them in what you call a sort of rest home. In this brief period of sleep and rest, the memory of the suffering and pain of dying, if they had a hard death, grows dim. They don't sleep until the resurrection, as the Church mistakenly has said, but only a few days or weeks. It all depends on how they come over.

"But most people who come over have no concept of what it's like, you know, and so they have to gradually be brought into the light, like a blind person. If he's blind for a long time and his sight is restored—well, you can't suddenly bring him into a glaring light. You have to gently bring him into it, so it won't hurt him."

What does it feel like when someone suddenly realizes he is dead? How does he appear to himself? Does he have a body?

Fletcher said: "In this world we all have perfect spiritual bodies. You know what St. Paul said, you have a spiritual body and a physical body and the two are not the same. And when you get rid of the physical, then you are in your spiritual body and it doesn't take on the aging or defects of the other."

The dead communicate among themselves by thought, said Fletcher, as they did with him in the periods when he took over control of Ford's mind and body during trance.

"The only time I use words is when I'm talking through Ford to people like you," Fletcher said. "Over here we do not use words. We use ideas, pictures, and symbols, and I have to interpret and put these into words for you to understand. But here we don't need words. Words get in the way."

What about heaven and hell?

Heaven, said Fletcher, and other mediumistic trance personalities, is a state of perpetual progress toward the perfect light of God. As for hell, a deceased Presbyterian pastor, purportedly communicating through Ford, said that hell is what we make it.

"There are people who come over here, who die, not knowing or believing anything, but who can still be taught, and these people can be brought into the light and into salvation. But I haven't found anyone yet who has gone to hell except a hell of his own creation.

"This hell is much worse, however, than anything the theologians can think of because it is a personal thing and the man realizes he's there because he has chosen it, don't you see?

"The hell of remorse is infinitely worse than physical punishment, believe me."

This same communicator, reporting his own alleged firsthand impressions, reflected a thought found in C. S. Lewis—that the obdurately wicked, as theologians used to call them, ultimately go out into a kind of extinction in which individual consciousness becomes a smear of nothingness in an inky void of unknowing. This may be the bottomless pit.

"I've been forced to the conclusion," said the Presbyterian pastor on the other side, "that there are some people who do not live after physical death because they deliberately chose not to. They turn their backs on God, they refuse to have any interest in anything of a spiritual nature, and while they live, they are in a sort of hell of their own making. . . . And there are people here who've been here a long time that we simply can't touch because they refuse even now to change their minds. They are convinced that there is nothing to life and, therefore, there is nothing for them, don't you see?"

The Living and the Dead

Some of Fletcher's most beautiful and suggestive thoughts were about the relationship between us, the so-called living, and those we call dead. There is not an impenetrable barrier between the two worlds, he said repeatedly, but a kind of spiritual membrane that permits a coming and going, quite apart from psychic experiments or séances, and even when we are totally unaware of it on the conscious level.

"The spirit world isn't a separate life from yours," a clergyman's deceased father said through the entranced Arthur Ford. "It interpenetrates your world.

"The way that the world you people live in appears to us is best described as you describe a foggy or cloudy day. That's the way your world looks to us. We are in the same place, really, but everything here is bathed in brilliant sunlight, while yours is, well, murky.

"We interpenetrate your world and we share it with you. If we like music, we can enjoy the music you play. If we want to go to church, we go to church and hear the sermons you hear. That's the communion of saints. . . ."

There is evidence that the afterlife, as a natural progression from this one, contains imperfections too which presumably are lost along the way as the spirit person progresses. There is no reason in logic, after all, why everybody suddenly should become perfect thinkers, writers, singers, or anything else merely because they have died.

Once I visited a man named Philip Watkins in the hospital; he was dying. Suddenly, while I sat by his bed, he roused, opened his eyes, turned to me, and said: "Don't you hear that chorus?"

I knew the man had been a Welsh miner for years and that like most of his countrymen, he loved to sing. His eyes bright, a smile touching his lips, he said he could hear a great choir now.

"Are they good?" asked a priest who was with me.

"Yes," said the dying man, "pretty good."

"How are the tenors?" asked the priest, knowing that the man was a tenor.

"Well," he replied after a pause, "they could be better."

A short time later the man died, the smile still on his face, lost in a music we couldn't hear, a music which, human-like, was good but not perfect.

The same idea—the communion of saints as a living reality—was brought home to me forcefully by an experience in a Ford sitting when suddenly, in the midst of totally unrelated material, the entranced medium said: "There's a person over here who says you know his parents. He was very young when he came over, but in his spirit body he looks older. Robert Seidel. He gives the name Robert Seidel.

"He says that his parents go to your church and that they are planning something for him. Something about an anniversary. Tell them not to worry any more and when they come to the altar that he says he will blend with them."

I knew the Seidel family as active members of the parish, but I wasn't aware of any deceased son. However, when I got back to my office I found the typed copy of the next week's church bulletin on my desk, and in the place customarily reserved for memorial flowers was listed the name Robert Seidel.

When I told the Seidels of my experience with Ford, and the message from their son, they received it with gratitude mixed with the usual, quite natural, puzzlement. They had planned to put the flowers on the altar, they said, because the coming Sunday was the anniversary of his death.

"Isn't it amazing that we should get such a message," said Mrs. Seidel. "We have always worried about Robert, who died as a baby, mainly because he was never baptized."

They came to Holy Communion that Sunday and, I am sure, felt the presence of their son as he "blended" with them. Communication and communion with our beloved dead are but two aspects of the same reality.

Fletcher once said that during the communion of discarnate minds with ours, especially at high moments of devotion, as during prayer or the Eucharist, benign influences seep into our souls.

"You see, said Fletcher, "when Jesus told the story about the scattering of the seeds, and some fell on good ground and some on stony ground, and some took root and some didn't—well, that's the way we work.

"The people we want to influence and help, we bombard with ideas, and that's what I mean by the throwing of seeds. If people are receptive, the seed takes root; they may not know that the idea comes from us, but it works out. Anyone who has been doing anything creative on the earth plane has been helped from this side.

"That's what Jesus meant by His parable. That's the way the Holy Spirit works by blending with your consciousness so that, if you're willing to be guided, you can be."

The concept of invisibles joining with us, the living, in our work and worship is not a new one really. It's inherent in the prayers invoking the angels, archangels, and all the company of heaven. It's inherent in all the references to our blessed dead and to the communion of saints.

It is this living intermingling of believers, seen and unseen, that dynamizes worship—not strobe lights, Coke-and-potato-chips communion services, jazz bands in the sanctuary, or other frenetic gimmickry aimed at evoking pseudoreligious euphoria.

One Lent, when I was ill, I had a shattering experience of the spiritual oneness of all believers, seen and unseen, the so-called dead and we, the so-called living.

Heavy with fever, from my room in the rectory I could hear the music coming from the church across the yard. Knowing the service so well, line by line, gesture by gesture, I could see clearly in my mind all that was happening. I heard the congregation's responses, and it was as though I were there.

Suddenly, time and space fell away. There, twenty years in the future, the same prayers, the same acts of faith—the same, untouched by time, eternal. Through all ages, I knew, and after, faith and love and service would remain always the same.

The inexpressible feeling that grasped me was beyond any human embodiment; it was beyond people, bigger than people, yet people were necessary to it.

Do our dead loved ones commune with us? Do they mingle their prayers with ours? Do they approach the same great altar of faith?

In that timeless moment I knew that the answer to these questions was an irresistible Yes.

Distilled from the experiences compressed into this chapter, here is my credo about mediumship and communication with the dead:

I believe that communication with our dead in Christ is possible and that it does occur.

I believe that mediumship, used for the glory of God and the service of man, is a noble calling, a divine gift.

I believe that the life we begin here continues hereafter and that, as Jesus said, whatsoever we sow, that shall we reap, here and hereafter.

I believe that the two worlds, this one and the next, interact; that the dead in Christ help us within the communion of saints as we, by our love and prayers, hasten them in their ascent to the light.

I believe in Life, not death.

8

ARTHUR FORD
The Triumph and the Tragedy . . .

One of the most painful experiences of my life was finding out that Arthur Ford cheated in his mediumship.

Oh, I had known for a long time that Arthur was no saint, even approximately (although he had his "saintly" moments). Almost from the beginning of our friendship his faults had loomed nearly as large as his virtues. Drinking was one of his serious problems, and there were others. But always I had believed that despite his weaknesses he maintained the integrity of his mediumship—until my traumatic discovery, that is.

It started one day during the research for Ford's biography (*Arthur Ford: The Man Who Talked with the Dead* [New York: New American Library, 1973]) on which Allen Spraggett and I collaborated. As Ford's literary legatee, after his death I received a hoard of his personal papers (though not all of them: An undisclosed amount was destroyed by a former secretary, presumably on Ford's instructions). It was while I was sifting through these papers that the moment of truth came.

Among the many newspaper clippings in Ford's files, including a suspiciously large number of obituaries (suspicious for a man whose business was bringing back the dead), I came across one from the New York *Times* with the heading: BISHOP BLOCK, 71, IS DEAD ON COAST.

Jolted, my fingers even trembling a little, I picked it up. What shook me was the fact that Bishop Karl Morgan Block of California, whose obituary it was, had been one of the alleged spirit communicators during the famous Bishop Pike-Arthur Ford television séance in 1967 when Pike said he believed he had contacted his dead son and others. Pike considered the message from Block, who had been his ecclesiastical predecessor, particularly impressive because it included rather obscure evidential details that the medium apparently couldn't have known.

Reading the obituary, however, I realized, with mounting shock, that every one of the small personal details about Bishop Block that Pike had found so "evidential" was mentioned! This clipping provided all the information Ford needed to convince Pike that Block had communicated.

There were other suspicious finds. After Ford's biography was published I came across another obituary in his papers, this one of a second prominent communicator in the Ford-Pike séance, the Reverend Lewis Pitt, rector of New York's Grace Church. Again, details that Bishop Pike had found evidential were mentioned in this New York *Times* obituary.

This is not the place to retell the story of how Allen Spraggett and I became fully convinced, after piecing together the evidence, that Arthur Ford had used fraud in his mediumship (that full story is recounted in *Arthur Ford: The Man Who Talked with the Dead,* which also tells why, after weighing all the facts, we concluded that Ford, though he sometimes cheated, nevertheless did have extraordinary psychic powers).

Why would a genuine medium stoop to fraud? Well why does a truthful man lie, an honest businessman cheat on his taxes, or a faithful husband commit adultery? The mystery of "mixed mediumship"—fact and fraud coexisting in the same medium—is just another example, though a peculiarly nasty one, of the ambiguity of human life and character in general.

No doubt some mediums who cheat would tell you it's merely to satisfy people's will to believe. And possibly some mediumistic fraud at least starts in this manner—by an attempt, that is, on the medium's part to make people feel good; to provide evidence when there is none; to avoid blank sittings; and, of course, by so doing to assure a satisfied clientele and healthy income for himself.

Later, if not sooner, however, the phony medium's character becomes so corrupted by habitual fraud that any relatively good motives are eroded and he loses even the ability to make moral judgments about his actions. He comes to believe that it's perfectly proper to lie, to invent messages, to pilfer information from purses and wallets, to do almost anything, if it's to help people believe.

This will to believe is used to cover a multitude of sins. The exposed fake medium is likely to ask: Who's really being hurt, anyway? Where is the harm in what I'm doing?

What Is the Prevalence of Mediumistic Fraud?

Permit me here a slight digression (though not a digression, really) to comment on the nature and prevalence of mediumistic fraud.

Occasional cheating by a genuine medium such as

Arthur Ford is one thing, and bad enough; but worse, with no mitigating features whatsoever, is the cold-blooded, systematic fraud practiced by mediumistic racketeers who, in most cases, are total cynics and have no more genuine psychic powers than the Amazing Kreskin.

Wholesale, organized mediumistic fraud exists. The sorry, shocking story is told in an explosive book, *The Psychic Mafia* (New York: Harper & Row, 1975), on which Allen Spraggett and I collaborated. This is the true story of a former fake medium, Lamar Keene, who tells all—the up-to-date files kept on prospective sitters, with personal information pilfered from a dozen sources; the electronic gadgets for "bugging" conversations to pick up evidential tidbits; the sordid sexual overtones, and sometimes overt acts, of certain phony mediums who specialize in a unique form of "grief therapy"; the welter of lies, deceit, and corruption in which the fraudulent psychic becomes immersed.

My personal experiences with mediumistic fraud of the organized variety have been—well, tragic or funny, depending on one's perspective. I have seen grown people oohing and ahing over some blatant piece of trickery that should have been apparent to a twelve-year-old. I've seen phony "ectoplasmic forms" (chiffon, really, stuck up the medium's nose or elsewhere) that were laughably fake—yet solemnly accepted by the believers as true spirit materializations. I've attended so-called "direct voice" sittings in which all the supposed spirit voices sounded like the medium with a bad cold. With skill, and not too much, really, almost anybody can duplicate the wondrous feats of the séance room fakes. A personal experience proved this.

One summer day I attended Camp Silver Belle, in Ephrata, Pennsylvania, a Spiritualist camp ground where the faithful go to commune with the departed for cash on the line. Marion and Allen Spraggett were with me. We wanted to see a medium named William Donnelly perform. He was said to be fantastic. Well, he was, but not in the way that was meant.

Donnelly, before a large congregation, demonstrated direct voice. First he drank a glass of milk, after saying that he would hold it in his mouth throughout the séance.

Then he had his mouth covered with a piece of adhesive tape by a member of the audience who penciled his initials on the tape so that they ran over onto the medium's skin. This was supposed to serve as a safeguard that the tape was not removed. The medium then entered a "cabinet," a small cubicle sealed off completely by black curtains, sat down in a chair, beside which stood a big aluminum trumpet (used by the spirits for their speaking), and the curtain was closed.

Eventually voices came from the cabinet. A procession of notables were heard from—John F. Kennedy, Madam Blavatsky, Mary Baker Eddy, and Paramahansa Yogananda, to name only some.

From where the Spraggetts were sitting, they could see a ray of light through a tiny rent in the black curtain, indicating that the medium had a pencil flashlight inside with him for script-reading purposes.

When the medium emerged from the cabinet he was still taped across the mouth. The same man who had written them examined the initials on the tape and said they showed no sign of having been tampered with. Then Donnelly removed the tape and into a glass spewed about the same quantity of milk he had taken into his mouth earlier.

There were gasps of astonishment from the crowd and then cyclonic applause, as the medium, looking very pleased with himself, took a bow.

Then we returned to the rectory in Woodbury and, in a private séance for the Spraggetts, I outdid the medium.

Putting up a makeshift cabinet, with a chair and an aluminum trumpet inside, I entered, seated myself and asked that my wrists and ankles be securely tied with rope, so that my hands were not free to manipulate anything. Then I drank most of a glass of milk. Following this, Allen Spraggett taped my mouth and penciled his initials across the tape.

In less than a minute, my spirit guide, "Mickey," who, I've been told, sounds remarkably like Mickey Mouse, spoke with greetings from various VIPs on the other side. A series of inane personal messages followed, culminating in the trumpet sailing over the top of the curtain. Yet when the curtains were opened a minute later, I was still tied hand and foot, my mouth securely taped, the initials in place. And when the tape was removed, I spewed most of a glass of milk out of my mouth.

How did I do it?

Simplicity itself. Well, almost. The rope-tying was meaningless, a mere blind. By straining against the ropes when they were being tied I got sufficient slack to allow me, when I later relaxed, to reach up with my hands and pull the tape away from my mouth. I was careful not to pull it all the way off, however; that would have disturbed the placement of the initials. I merely pulled the tape down enough for me to speak but leaving the penciled initials intact.

The milk in my mouth? Simple. I swallowed it, of course, then replaced it with milk sucked up through a straw from a vial hidden inside my shirt.

Voilà! A direct-voice séance in which the spirits not only spoke while the medium was bound hand and foot and his mouth full of milk but even hurled the trumpet out of the cabinet!

A Hoax Perpetrated

The real *tour de force* of my brief career as a phony medium came when I presided over a séance before a group of members of a respected psychic research society. The society's executive committee was in on the hoax, the purpose of which was to provide the members with a vivid object lesson in the methods of fake mediums.

I was introduced by the society's president as the newly discovered and no doubt soon-to-be-famous English sensitive, Donald Bennett, a protégé (it was mentioned) of the distinguished University of Edinburgh parapsychologist, Professor Temple Herzog.

Affecting an ever-so-slightly-British accent and a modest demeanor, I told the group (about 150 people) that recently I had developed one of the rarest of psychic phenomena: "independent voice." Under strict test conditions, which would be duplicated tonight, I promised, spirit voices were heard in my séances. These voices were audible to everybody and usually conveyed evidential information, I added.

Then the president of the society (one of my coconspirators, of course) had me drink a glass of milk, taped my mouth, and scribbled his initials across the tape, then led me to my "cabinet," which contained only a plain wooden chair. To the recorded strains of Wagner's "Ride of the Valkyrie," the curtain was drawn and the house lights were dimmed.

In a few moments, from behind the curtain, above the surging music, came the shrill voice of "Sydney," Donald Bennett's cockney spirit guide. He greeted the sitters (from whom there were appropriate murmurs of surprise that a voice should be heard speaking from a cabinet containing a gagged medium). Then Sydney introduced other spirit communicators.

Five distinctly different spirit voices were heard by the sitters—one purporting to be that of the late Canadian Prime Minister and spiritualist, Mackenzie King—and these conveyed evidential items of information. One sitter, whom the medium had never met, was told the name of his favorite professor in medical school; another heard from a high school friend who had died twenty years before; a third was told her childhood nickname.

When the lights were turned up and I (alias Donald Bennett) emerged from the cabinet, mouth still taped, there was a buzz of excitement in the audience. When the president attested that his initials on the tape were still intact, then removed the tape and I spewed nearly a glassful of milk from my mouth, there was prolonged applause.

In the question-and-answer period that followed, it was evident that many of the group were convinced they had witnessed genuine psychic phenomena. One woman stood and in a voice tremulous with emotion said: "Mr. Bennett, this has been an unforgettable experience for us." A man reported having seen spirit faces hovering over my cabinet during the séance.

Then a gray-haired, steely-eyed lady, past middle age, a former tax inspector (as I discovered later), arose and in clipped tones asked: "Who wrote this scenario? I smell a rat."

The tone of her question caused a commotion in the audience. Some were evidently embarrassed by her skepticism. At this point, dropping my British accent, I said: "Ladies and gentlemen, you have been the victims of fraud. I am not Donald Bennett the medium but William Rauscher, an Episcopal priest."

Every year, thousands of people across the United States are bilked by racketeering psychic parasites. As a

priest and a psychic investigator, I warn you: Beware of
fraudulent mediums!

What shocked me even more than the revelation of
Arthur Ford's cheating was that some of his ardent admirers, who no doubt considered themselves seekers after
truth, demanded that the truth about his mediumistic
misdemeanors be suppressed. What good would it do,
they pleaded, to reveal that Arthur Ford and other genuine mediums sometimes cheated?

This attitude, so far as I'm concerned, is perilously close
to that of the fake medium himself who cloaks his deceit
in the guise of protecting the faith of the little old ladies
who believe in him.

As a priest writing an honest book, a truthful book,
about the psychic, I cannot take this attitude of easy
tolerance. It is important for honest seekers to know
about the dark side of the psychic world.

Too, my present opportunity is my only one to set
down some very personal impressions of that flawed
giant, Arthur Ford: his triumphs, which were magnificent,
and his tragedies, which, in their own way, were almost
as awesome. We can profit from an honest consideration
of both.

Portrait of a Medium as a Young Man

Arthur Ford was born on January 8, 1897, in Titusville,
Florida, and in childhood gave little enough indication
of being a psychic genius. Raised in a strict Baptist home,
as a boy he showed more interest in Sunday school than
in séances.

It was before he was nine years old, Ford said, that he
came to know the boy who much later was to assume the
role of codweller of his body—Fletcher, his ghostly friend

and mentor. Fletcher was one of a French-Canadian family whom Ford last saw as a child (at least, according to the authorized version of his life story; in other, less formal accounts there were some differences).

It was many years after their last "earthly" meeting, when Ford was twenty-seven and a Disciples of Christ minister developing mediumship, that one day, in trance, an invisible personality announced himself and said: "Tell Ford I'll be with him from now on." Asked about himself, the newcomer disclosed that he was the medium's childhood friend who had been killed, he informed them, while serving with the Canadian Army in World War I. He confided that he would go by his middle name, "Fletcher," to avoid possibly embarrassing his family, who were devout Catholics and many of whose ideas (such as that only Catholics go to the nice place) he had found to be untrue.

So began the Ford-Fletcher partnership, which lasted more than forty years and took the medium around the world, into the salons of the rich and the halls of the mighty.

During the 1930s, Arthur Ford was the foremost public exponent of American Spiritualism and its ambassador to many other countries, notably England, where he made several triumphal tours. And they were indeed triumphal. Ford's first visit to England earned him the admiration and patronship of Sir Arthur Conan Doyle, creator of Sherlock Holmes and an ardent Spiritualist. Ford overwhelmed the British with the brilliance of his clairvoyance, and newspaper reports indicate that it wasn't only Spiritualists he impressed. A British reporter described a Ford demonstration as "the most amazing, inexplicable thing I have ever seen."

One of the people Ford met in Britain was another psychic, his female counterpart as the royalty of mediumship, Eileen Garrett. A colorful, dynamic lady, with a personality every bit as complex and elusive as Ford's, and with greater intellectual acumen than he, she and the young American became immediate friends and life-long enemies. There was between them all their days a love-hate. (Mrs. Garrett was a witness at Ford's second marriage, and when that broke up by divorce, she and Arthur drifted apart; during the last years they never saw each other, though much of the time they lived only a hundred miles apart, she in New York and he in Philadelphia.)

It was Eileen Garrett, herself one of the great mediums of all time, dubbed by some "the high priestess of the paranormal," who spoke of Arthur sardonically as "that rising and falling angel."

"How is the bad boy?" she would ask me of him, with the mixture of elfin charm and almost sinister guile—a quality of "depraved innocence," one observer called it —which was characteristic of her in her later years.

For his part, Arthur, when I mentioned Eileen, would snap: "Well, how is the old bitch?"

Really, it took an Eileen Garrett, someone who herself had plumbed the depths of mediumship, to know an Arthur Ford. She understood, as could only another psychic, and one who, like Ford, had enjoyed international attention, the terrible stresses that mediumship puts on moral character: The constant flattery of those who want to know the unknown; the seductiveness of the money and other favors offered in return for special revelations; and the insidious, ever-present temptation for the medium, especially when psychic results aren't as good as expected, to give the spirits a helping hand with a little cheating.

Eileen also knew the emotional storms that can rage within the medium's psyche because of his unusual psychological makeup. Everyone may be psychic (and is, I believe, in the same sense that everybody has *some* musical talent), but not everyone can do the things an Arthur Ford or an Eileen Garrett did. Manifestly, then, these people are different.

Mrs. Garrett admitted to me once that, yes, sex was part of mediumship, and who should be surprised at that? The energy for mediumship, as for most creative endeavors, she noted, is drawn from the sexual centers. It was hard for her to imagine a powerful medium who wasn't also energized by a powerful libido.

A Life Menaced and Acclaimed

Great psychics often have exhibited personality problems. Many have had messy private lives, and sometimes have come to abject, unhappy ends. They possessed the gift of helping others without, seemingly, being able to help themselves. This, in essence, was the tragedy of Arthur Ford. "Others he saved, himself he could not save."

But though often morose, Ford wasn't always so; on the contrary. If the mood was right, he had enough charm to be the life of a dozen parties. He was a great character, as mediums usually are. One of the things about them that attracts me is their streak of lovable madness, their zaniness, and Arthur must have been the maddest and zaniest of them all.

He was, for example, absolutely the world's worst driver. That he survived his periodic forays on the highway probably was due to Fletcher, certainly not to Ford. We had some hair-raising experiences as he drove, always at high speed, straight down the white line on a main highway, puffing on his cigar and talking all the while, oblivious of the other cars blowing their horns and veering out of his way.

Once, when I was with him in the car, another driver yelled: "Where the hell did you get your license?" Arthur, without slackening his speed for a moment or modifying his erratic course, looked over his shoulder and remarked innocently: "You know, a guy like that is a menace on the road."

He was quick on the quip, and many of them were gently self-deprecating. When I asked him once how he was getting to a lecture, he said: "No problem, my new broom just arrived." In a foul mood, he could snap: "I wouldn't give a sitting to the Virgin Mary!"

When Arthur got drunk he was either very funny or very nasty, or sometimes both. Once I answered the phone at his apartment and a cultured voice said that this was the Reverend Mr. So-and-So, and did I know what Mr. Ford's lecture topic would be so it could be printed before he spoke at this gentleman's church? Arthur, who had overheard, grabbed the phone and barked: "Yeah, I'll tell you his subject: *Screw 'em all!* How's that for a title?" With that, he hung up.

There was Ford's fund of funny stories, all true. He gave a spirit message at a meeting to a woman whom he knew to be some sort of sectarian clergy, so he addressed her: "Reverend . . ." She replied, a little testily: "I'm not a reverend, I'm an archbishop!" When Ford, ever the gentleman, said politely: "Then, your Grace," the woman cut in: "My name ain't Grace!"

When he was in his cups Arthur could bemoan the fact that all people wanted from him was his psychic talent.

"I have to sit for my supper," he lamented, "wherever I go."

It was true that many hosts seemed to expect him to give a séance, as though he were an amateur magician doing a few tricks at a party.

"Sure," he sulked to me once, "I get plenty of invitations to parties and I'm a hit when I'm there. But I always leave alone."

Though dramatized and overdone, his complaints had

to them a certain poignant truth. As a great psychic, Arthur was feted, acclaimed, lionized. He gave sittings for royalty: Queen Maud of Norway, for example, bestowed on him a diamond signet ring as a token of her appreciation. He rubbed shoulders with the literati, such as novelists Aldous Huxley and Upton Sinclair, who rhapsodized over his mediumship (Sinclair used Ford as the model for a character, a clairvoyant, in one of his Lanny Budd novels). In his salad days Ford was mentioned in New York gossip columns as the swain of Broadway stars. But, as he said, it was his psychic ability that attracted the admirers and he was human enough, like others who are popular for what they do instead of necessarily for their own sakes, to resent the lionizing even as he enjoyed it.

Though Ford joined Alcoholics Anonymous and credited it with bringing him to "a second conversion," he never beat his drinking problem. It ravaged him in more ways than one—physically, mentally, morally, spiritually. Yet in spite of it, and this is a mark of his greatness, he rose to heights of which few mediums even dream. Obviously one cannot compress so rich and diverse a character as Arthur Ford into the pages of a chapter, or even a book, but, before moving on to other subjects, let us consider two very important issues: the seriousness and weight of the evidence that Ford sometimes cheated in his mediumship; and the question of whether this evidence compromises his mediumship as a whole and undermines any confidence in it.

The Impact of Revelations

When the biography of Ford was published, with its revelations that he probably cheated in the Ford-Pike séance, a lot of hell (if not quite all) broke loose.

The book, mind you, does not assert that Ford was a

cheat, period. It offers the painful evidence that on occasion—how often nobody knows—he did resort to fraud. That he also had genuine psychic powers, however, is documented in the book—incontestably, to my mind. To be sure, Ford was no simple cheat, no mere trickster, no two-bit occult poseur. He was a great psychic—but not all the time.

I expected strong reactions to the book from some of Arthur's friends and admirers. I was one of them, after all, and it had been devastating for me to face the evidence that Ford cheated. (Spraggett and I came to the conclusion of proven fraud, by the way, on the basis of varied data: the numerous suspicious obituaries in Ford's files; the fragment we found of what appeared to be a notebook containing biographical data on sitters; and the testimony of several people, including Arthur's former secretary, that he had admitted to them that he practiced fraud. The former secretary said that Ford carried a Gladstone suitcase containing his notes on people when he went to a sitting.)

I had hoped, however, that once the initial shock of the revelations wore off, mature admirers of Arthur would recognize, as I had, that while the fraud cast a shadow on his mediumship, it by no means totally discredited it.

What dismayed me was the utterly emotional, even hysterical reaction from some of Ford's followers, who contended that the unfavorable evidence should have been suppressed. They wanted to hide the truth—in the interests of truth, of course.

But it disturbed me because I realized now, more than before, how widespread an affliction it is—this desire to suppress the truth when it hurts; to go to any lengths to protect a cult image, even when that image is a false one.

Arthur Ford, great man though he was, was no stained-glass saint, and in his better moments he was the first to admit it. He would have had contempt, I'm sure, for the cultist practices of some of his followers, who, for example, after his death and cremation kept fragments of his bones, presumably as sacred relics.

There were other, more wholesome reactions to the Ford book.

In a letter to me headed "Parapsychology: problems of a great art form," Dr. Humphrey Osmond, noted psychiatrist and psychical researcher, commented on the New York *Times* piece about the book and Ford's cheating. His remarks were a wise commentary on the problem of fraud in mediumship.

"I remember," Dr. Osmond wrote, "Mrs. Eileen Garrett mentioning this unfortunate habit of Arthur Ford's some years before her death. I found this distressing and have often thought about it since then.

"It seems to me that the problem becomes easier to understand if one looks upon this kind of mediumship as an art form, rather than some less personal activity."

All artists—writers, painters, orators—have off days, said Dr. Osmond, and mediums surely are no exception. The temptation at such times to fake it, to fill in, must be enormous.

In mediumship, as in singing or acting, the problem, Dr. Osmond said, is the same: "Great performances cannot be commanded."

He observed, too, that in many cases a genuine medium may use cheating to warm up the audience and stimulate the flow of real psychic perceptions. "Success of a genuine kind can probably be primed, started up, with what amounts to a bit of fraud," he said.

There were some who knew Arthur, both the bright and the shadow side of his character, and believed that his gifts were big enough to survive the truth. One of these, William Luce, in reply to a Florida woman's attack, wrote to the executive council of Spiritual Frontiers Fellowship (SFF) a spirited and informed defense of the

Ford biography, in which he affirmed he personally knew that Ford sometimes cheated.

"I want to speak in support of Mr. Rauscher and Mr. Spraggett," wrote Mr. Luce. "Their book is an honest and extremely well-written biography. It handles sensitive areas of Arthur's character and career kindly and fairly without glossing over facts. It doesn't personalize his sexual life. His possible resort to researching sitters in the last years—when he was fighting alcoholism and illness —should be no lasting shock to people who, by the time they join SFF, are presumably acquainted with the psychology of mediums."

Of Ford's habit of researching sitters, Mr. Luce said: "Incidentally, when I was staying with Arthur in December 1970, he gave me some keys and asked me to look for the SFF bound volume of his trance sittings—which he gave me. During the search I came upon the obituaries— piles of them—in one of the trunks. A very significant conversation ensued, which I won't go into now. The only point I want to make is that I saw them. And he wanted me to see them."

Mr. Luce went on to praise Arthur for his genuine psychic gifts and his human qualities.

This kind of response to the whole truth about Arthur Ford seems to me the mature and wise one; and, for an honest person, ultimately the only possible one.

Decisive Evidence

But now to a final and important question: What significance have these revelations of occasional cheating for the general credibility of Ford's mediumship? What, for example, about the sittings cited in this book? Were the messages real or invented? Doesn't the knowledge that he sometimes cheated tend to discredit Ford's medium-ship as a whole?

Well, as you may imagine, being cognizant of Ford's unfortunate propensity made me critically examine the incidents from his mediumship cited in this book. For me, they stand the test of the most critical judgment. In virtually every case, Ford's good faith need not be assumed. There is no evident way that he could have cheated. The information, by its nature, was not accessible to research. Therefore, we are justified in accepting it as valid evidence.

This was true, moreover, of much of Ford's work. To show, as decisively as it's possible to do so, that Arthur Ford could and did produce facts not normally known, let me offer three special cases in which prior research is ruled out—in the first, because there was a precognitive element, and the information, since it lay in the future, couldn't be known to anybody; and in the second and third, because the information was so idiosyncratic that research seems unthinkable.

In September 1962, four young people had a psychic session with Arthur Ford at my rectory. Taking a personal object belonging to each one (a watch, ring, and medal), the medium proceeded to "psychometrize" it—pick up psychically information about the owner. Ford had met none of the young people, yet his predictions for them proved to be astonishingly accurate, not merely in general terms but in specifics, including names meaning-less to them at the time.

Ford said that he saw one young lady in white and that she would be a nurse. A young man, who was then entering his college sophomore year, he said he saw as a clergyman. A second young man he saw in an Air Force uniform of blue and remarked that someone named Eldridge would have an influence on him. The fourth young person, a girl, he said he could see wearing white and working in a laboratory, but she wasn't happy and should quit and do what she really wanted to do.

Two of these young people later wrote me about their subsequent careers and how eerily prescient Ford had been.

The young lady whom Ford saw in white, as a nurse, later took nursing and eventually joined the staff at Pennsylvania State Hospital. The other young lady, whom he had seen in a lab, unhappy, indeed was working in one at that time and *was* unhappy. Taking the medium's suggestion to do what she really wanted, she quit her lab job and went into nursing.

The college sophomore, whom Ford said would become a clergyman, did, though at the time of the prediction his future career was up in the air. Most interesting of all, the other young man, whom Ford had seen in a blue uniform, entered Valley Forge Military Academy and, on walking around the grounds, was astonished to discover a plaque in memory of a former chaplain at the school, a certain Eldridge Walker. "Eldridge," remember, was the name of somebody whom Ford predicted would be an influence in this boy's life.

In a letter to me the young man said of the deceased Eldridge Walker: "Recently I ran across another plaque I had overlooked, in memory of Walker and with a list of his activities which, more or less rationally, I could say pertained to me. He was, among other things, dean of admissions at the junior college I attend, Chaplain, a teacher of history, and then professor of history. To me it came as quite a surprise or even a shock."

The young man recalled Ford had predicted that the "Eldridge" mentioned would have an influence on his choice of a vocation; he was planning, he said, to major in history.

The Reverend Paul Lambourne Higgins, Methodist minister and first president of Spiritual Frontiers Fellowship, knew Arthur Ford well and had many sittings with him. Mr. Higgins received much evidential material—more than enough, he says—to convince him that the medium truly was contacting the dead. One of the most convincing bits of evidence, from the standpoint of whether or not it could conceivably have been researched, was another of those "tremendous trifles." It concerned—well, let Mr. Higgins tell the story.

"The sitting was in Chicago on December 6, 1953," he recalls. "In bringing to me a message from my mother, calling her Minnie Hauk, her maiden name, Ford said, 'When her body was buried you put on her dress a little cameo; this is her sign to you now. . . .'

"Nobody then alive, except myself, could have known the meaning of this message. When I was a little boy one of the first gifts I ever bought for my mother with my own allowance was a cameo, which she always cherished.

"Years later, when she passed on, we did not have a wake, for this was her request, but before the casket was taken to the church for the service I pinned on her dress the little cameo."

In 1961, shortly after I became rector of Christ Church, Woodbury, Fletcher gave me a communication that purported to be from the Right Reverend Paul Matthews, a deceased former bishop of New Jersey.

The bishop said that he knew my predecessor, Canon Robert G. W. Williams, well, and was happy that I had succeeded so fine a priest and that now Christ Church was my parish. He added: "Bobby has my cross." "Bobby" I took to mean Canon Williams.

A little while later, after the canon's death, his wife said to me: "Bill, I want you to have Bobby's cross."

Then, for some reason, she added: "He always wore it; Bishop Matthews gave it to him, you know."

I confess that my breath caught for an instant. How, I asked myself, could Arthur Ford have known this very personal fact about the canon? My answer then, as it is today, was that such information most likely came from the one who knew: the dead bishop who had given him the cross.

Ford's Relationship with Fletcher

Arthur Ford, in spite of his failings, had, I'm convinced, a genuine belief in and affection for his spirit guide, Fletcher. Whether Fletcher was or was not an actual discarnate spirit, a split-off fragment of Ford's own deep self, or some sort of transcendental personality from the collective unconscious (all theories that have been offered) is not really crucial to the issue here, which is the medium's own attitude to Fletcher. Ford took him seriously. The most striking evidence of this were those times when Ford gave a sitting for himself—that is, went into a trance and let somebody else ask Fletcher questions on his behalf.

Once, when Bob Lewis and I were with him, Ford had a "vision" during his sleep that disturbed him—so much, in fact, that he summoned us and demanded that we talk to Fletcher for him there and then, with no delays.

Ford went into trance, with some difficulty; the process seemed labored, the breathing more rasping than usual, the bodily twitches more pronounced. Then Fletcher came through and greeted us.

"What kind of experience did Ford have that so upset him?" Bob Lewis asked.

"I've been told about it," Fletcher said calmly, matter-of-factly. "I didn't have anything to do with it. There are different levels of beings over here, just as on the earth plane. You can make the general statement that all of us here are angels, but different kinds of angels—grades, a hierarchy. And when some of the more advanced people find it necessary to return, it is for a purpose, but a purpose that those of us on the lower level find hard to understand.

"Just as I have a vehicle by which I speak to you—that is, Ford—so the higher beings above me use vehicles to descend to us. . . ."

Then Fletcher went on to interpret Ford's unsettling vision as an admonition to him to live a better life so as to better serve mankind.

"Ford must demonstrate in his own person the things he preaches and teaches to others. He must be constant. He must not break his word. He must keep his vows. In the act of doing that, he will be given the strength that is necessary."

This was an evident reference to the fact that Arthur earlier had confided that he planned to cancel a number of speaking engagements for which he had given commitments.

"The law is: You cannot get help from our side if you refuse to fulfill your obligation on every level where you are now," Fletcher concluded.

On awakening, and being told Fletcher's remarks, Ford was silent for a while, then announced that he wasn't going to cancel those speaking engagements after all.

Arthur Ford died on the night of January 4, 1971, after a series of heart attacks. His last words were, "God help me."

Almost immediately after his death, in Miami, those who wanted to make a cult figure out of him began their bizarre rituals. At the funeral home where his body lay, a newspaper reporter arrived to find two people huddled in the corner doing automatic writing. The day before, a woman admirer had sat at the piano in the funeral home and played the wedding march! To myself I said:

"If Arthur could be heard now he would shout, 'Get the hell out of here, you damn fools!'"

The funeral was held on Thursday, January 7, in Christ Congregational Church, Miami, where the Reverend T. N. Tiemeyer, a friend of Ford's and a former SFF council member, was pastor. He and I shared the service, which was simple and reverent. Both of us spoke, and another SFF council member, the Reverend Harlan C. Musser, also participated.

Prior to the service, Ford's body, as he had requested, was cremated. On Saturday morning, Clem Tamburrino rented a boat and went out into the Atlantic some miles from shore and there scattered Arthur Ford's mortal remains.

But not all of Ford's mortal remains were consigned to the sea. Later, to my shock, I discovered that some of the medium's devotees had kept fragments of his bones as—what, holy objects? Through my efforts and insistence, these last remnants of Arthur's mortal shell found a fitting resting place, causing me to make this notation in my parish register:

"I, William V. Rauscher, Priest, Canon, and Rector of Christ Church, Woodbury, New Jersey, did inter on sacred ground the additional cremated remains of the medium

ARTHUR FORD
(1896–1971)

at 12:00 noon on Saturday, August 18, 1973.

"A secret place, never to be revealed, was provided in the earth for the ashes brought to me by a friend and prayers were offered.

"May his soul find peace."

9

THE
PARAPSYCHOLOGY
OF PRAYER

When Air Canada Flight 831 to Toronto left Montreal International Airport on the evening of November 29, 1963, Leonard J. Crimp was supposed to be on board.

That day, five friends of Mr. Crimp, unknown to each other, had phoned his wife inquiring about him. Each confessed to having a strange feeling that Mr. Crimp was in danger. Told that he was away on a trip, all said they felt a compulsion to pray for him.

Four minutes after the takeoff of Flight 831, the huge DC-8 jetliner plunged to earth and exploded in a ball of fire a hundred feet high. All 118 persons on board were killed. But Leonard Crimp was not among them.

By a curious twist of circumstances—so curious that Mr. Crimp, a devout Christian layman, called it a "miracle"—he missed the fatal flight. Here is the story of that miracle.

The Story of a Miracle

Leonard Crimp was slated to retire early in 1964 as sales vice president of H. J. Heinz of Canada, Ltd. As one of his last official duties, he accompanied his successor, forty-eight-year-old John M. Page, on a tour of the company's national sales force.

In the early evening of the fateful day, the two men arrived in Montreal on a flight from Canada's East Coast. They were scheduled to connect in Montreal with Air Canada Flight 851 to Toronto, but their arrival was delayed by bad weather and that flight had left.

A ground hostess told the twelve Toronto-bound passengers that arrangements had been made for them to take Flight 831, which was to leave for Toronto in thirty minutes. She asked the group to follow her to Gate 41 for boarding.

"We were then at Gate 5," Mr. Crimp said in an interview, "and the twelve of us fell in behind the hostess for the long walk to Gate 41.

"We were almost there when the hostess suddenly asked, 'Is Mr. Crimp in this group?' When I identified myself she said, 'There's a seat for you on Flight 277 at Gate 7.'

"Frankly, I was peeved. I knew that Flight 277 was a prop-driven plane, a Viscount, and I wanted the faster, smoother jet. I protested, but the hostess insisted. She suggested that I let my baggage go on Flight 831 and said it would arrive in Toronto the same time I did.

"So, grumbling, I admit, I told my companion I would meet him in Toronto and started back to Gate 7."

When Leonard Crimp attempted to board the plane at Gate 7, an attendant snapped: "Where did you come from?" When he explained that there was supposed to be a seat for him, the man growled, "How confused can they get?" However, after a phone call he gave Mr. Crimp a boarding pass, and the Viscount took off almost immediately.

On arriving in Toronto, Mr. Crimp went straight to a business meeting. It was not until several hours later, about 10 P.M., that he phoned his wife and heard from her about the crash of Flight 831.

"I was stunned," he said. "I couldn't believe it. Then I began to wonder about the strange thing that had happened to me."

Leonard Crimp had no idea why he had been singled out by the hostess to take that earlier flight. But as a Christian, he believed something more than sheer chance was involved.

"My life is in God's hands," he stated during an interview, "and I believe that I was spared for a purpose."

Fortunate "Coincidences"—or Prayers Answered?

As evidence that his escape was more than coincidence, Mr. Crimp cited the five friends who independently called his wife the day of the crash to inquire about him. All confessed to being strangely concerned about him, though they couldn't say why. When told that he was on a business trip, they said they had a compulsion to pray for him.

For me, this is a remarkable example of the parapsychology of prayer—how a human petition can transcend the limitations of the physical senses to accomplish its benign purposes. The individuals who sensed that Leonard Crimp was in danger no doubt were psychically attuned to him, even without knowing it, and precognitively picked up the impending disaster. Their prayers probably set in motion the curious chain of events that saved his life.

How many fortunate "coincidences," I wonder, are rooted in somebody's praying? How much of fate is engineered by prayer?

Archbishop William Temple once said: "When I pray, coincidences happen. When I stop praying, the coincidences don't happen."

And it was another archbishop of Canterbury, Geoffrey Fisher, who said about space travel: "Of course I believe in it. I travel through space every day when I pray."

In prayer, we reach out beyond ourselves—vertically to God and horizontally to other people. The outreach of prayer, working through mysterious psychic channels, can perform what men sometimes call miracles.

Leonard Crimp's dramatic escape from death raises, of course, profound and painful questions (which, however, belong more to the theology than to the parapsychology of prayer). Why was Mr. Crimp spared and not the others on the plane? If there was some inscrutable purpose in his deliverance, was there also purpose in the others' deaths? And if so, what could it be?

These questions are insoluble. The only possible answers are the provisional ones of faith. But the issue finally boils down to this: Either Leonard Crimp's experience, and others like it, was pure chance (in which case God presumably had nothing to do with it), or it was a part of divine providence (in which case God had everything to do with it).

For me, as a Christian, only the latter answer is possible. And as a psychical investigator, I grasp that Leonard Crimp's experience falls into a familiar pattern.

Psychical literature bristles with cases of "crisis telepathy" in which a person in danger, though sometimes unaware of it, apparently sends out a call for help that is picked up by others tuned into his particular wavelength.

In the case of Leonard Crimp, prayer adds a magnificent new dimension. His concerned friends, the unconscious telepathic receivers, turned their concern into prayer, thereby (as I believe) setting in motion, possibly through psychokinesis, the chain of events that saved his life.

When we pray, we broadcast. It was this that led Nandor Fodor, a noted psychoanalyst, to say: "I believe that the substance of prayer is this: A human anguish spreads all over the universe and may get an answer from the Cosmic Mind."

Prayer as Consciousness-Raising

The alternative to believing that prayer really makes an objective difference, that it can change things outside the person, is to believe that it's simply a monologue, a sort of spiritual weight-lifting by which we build our own moral muscles but with no direct effect on anybody or anything beyond ourselves. Now, to be sure, prayer *is* a powerful form of self-suggestion and can legitimately be used this way—as in healing. But it's more than talking to our deeper self. Mighty forces are mobilized and unleashed by prayer, objective forces which, in Jesus' phrase, can cast mountains into the sea.

Essentially, however, prayer is not petitionary, not asking. Rather, it is a method of consciousness-raising. Prayer is the way by which we direct our consciousness to a higher source. It involves thought with inward and/or outward action in which the person praying tries to invoke a response from his God.

This response may be in the form of guidance, healing, communion, revelation, a sense of oneness, or aid for departed friends or loved ones; for in prayer, make no mistake, we embrace the so-called dead as well as the so-called living.

Petitionary prayer—"asking" prayer—valid though it is, represents only the bottom rung of the spiritual ladder. Prayer is in essence mystical. That doesn't mean spooky or occult. The word "mystical" has nothing to do with hearing voices or seeing visions; in fact, the great mystics of all traditions, Christian and non-Christian, shunned these things as mere distractions from the main business of prayer, which is getting to know God.

Mystical prayer is a sort of time-exposure of the soul to God in which we open ourselves to the divine presence so that, as on a sensitive photographic film, His image may be imprinted on us.

The highest form of prayer is pure offering. It is praise. And though this kind of prayer seeks and asks nothing except God's presence, it often bears practical fruit. In fact, it is precisely this mystical prayer that liberates the greatest power.

Kathryn Kuhlman, the celebrated charismatic healer, told me one secret she has discovered is that praise is powerful.

"When we praise the Lord," she said, "not asking Him for a single thing, that's when the healings start. It's praise that brings the Holy Spirit."

Psychic Personalities—People of Prayer

The greatest psychic personalities I have known have been people of prayer.

Jeane Dixon begins each day with attendance at Mass. The London medium Ena Twigg speaks of the reality of her prayer experiences. Rosemary Brown, the medium who receives music from dead composers, prays before every psychic session to sensitize herself to the spirits.

Arthur Ford prayed. The minister of Philadelphia's Arch Street Methodist Church, the Reverend James

Haney, said that the famed medium often popped into the sanctuary to sit quietly alone, meditating. Eileen Garrett, another great medium, spoke of "blending with all living things, all life," which I consider a mystical experience. London's society clairvoyant Tom Corbett regularly attends St. Mary Magdalene, Bildeston, Suffolk.

Edgar Mitchell, the Apollo 14 astronaut, sixth man to walk on the moon, told me how, standing on the lunar surface and gazing at planet Earth, he was overwhelmed by what he called a "eureka experience" and I would call an attitude of prayer. In that timeless moment, he said, seeing the Earth as a tiny ball floating in the immensity of space, his consciousness was stretched to global dimensions. He felt an inexpressible longing to help men realize their oneness with each other and their potential for growth as children of the cosmos.

For Edgar Mitchell, that moment remains a perspective from which to judge the rest of life. And so with all of us: Prayer moments are our best moments, representing touchstones against which to test all other moments.

Since prayer annuls time and space, it ignores death, and so we pray for the dead. And do they pray for us? I believe they do and that all our prayers—those of the incarnate and discarnate alike—mingle before the throne of God.

The efficacy of prayer on behalf of the dead is shown in the unique ministry of my friend the Reverend Canon John Pearce-Higgins, who "deghosts" haunted houses with a special service of requiem. He concludes the service with this lovely old prayer: "O thou unquiet spirit, who at thy departure from the contagions of the flesh chosest to remain earthbound and to haunt this place, go thy way rejoicing that the prayers of the faithful shall follow thee, that thou mayest enjoy everlasting rest, and mayest find thy rightful place at the Throne of Grace, through Jesus Christ our Lord. . . .

"Rest eternal grant unto them O Lord, and let light perpetual shine upon them as Thou promised of old unto Abraham and to his seed. Amen."

A case that involved prayer links between this world and the next occurred in 1967. That was when Everett Wallis, a professor of chemistry at Princeton and a devout Episcopal layman whom I had met at diocesan conventions, suddenly died. His wife was grief-stricken, particularly since his death came not long after the death of the Wallis's son.

Mrs. Wallis told me how, after her husband's passing, she moved out of the big house in Princeton into a small apartment. Loneliness was her only companion. Though a person of deep faith, she sometimes experienced moods of utter bleakness. There seemed no purpose at all in the deaths of her husband and son. In spite of her efforts to believe, faith ebbed.

One day, at emotional rock bottom, Mrs. Wallis knelt in her kitchen and, feeling as though her life depended on it, prayed: "O God, help me. I need help. Help me."

Almost while she was still praying, the phone rang. It was a friend whom Mrs. Wallis hadn't heard from in months. The friend said: "I just had to call you. Something told me to do it this moment. The truth is that I've been wondering how to tell you something because, frankly, I have no idea how you'll take it. You see, my husband and I went to a medium and there was a message for you. From Everett."

Mrs. Wallis made an appointment with the same medium. What came through in that sitting satisfied her of her husband's and son's survival of death. Names of her husband's professional colleagues and her son's friends were cited, and even a description of a strange dream and vision that Mrs. Wallis had experienced after her son's death. The evidence was irresistibly convincing.

Her husband concluded his message through the medium with the assurance that his thoughts and feelings mingled with hers in prayer, especially at Holy Communion.

"We are never as close to people as we are in prayer," he said. "When you kneel at the altar rail, not only Jesus is there but all those who have never really left you."

In prayer we escape from the four walls of our small self into the vast wonders and beauty of God's spiritual universe.

10

PSYCHIC PROBLEMS

Possession,

Automatic Writing,

and Other Exotica

In the realm of psychic experience, as in any other area of life, people can have problems.

Sometimes these are relatively minor, psychic measles or indigestion, as it were; but they can take more serious, occasionally even malignant forms.

Often the psychic problem has elements that make it appear to others, though rarely if ever to the victim, not only bizarre but funny. Psychic problems, as problems, are no funnier than any others, but the behavior of the people who have them often is a good deal funnier than other peoples'. The sheer craziness of some of this behavior represents one side of what I call the mad, mad world of the psychic.

(To be sure, if I may digress for a moment, not all the high humor of the psychic centers on its problems. Much of it springs from the very nature of the subject— for example, the unconscious remarks of mediums and

psychics. I remember walking with Jeane Dixon, the celebrated seeress, in Washington, D.C., when she glanced
at a newspaper headline announcing some startling event
in world affairs and remarked matter-of-factly: "Oh, I
could have told them that"; or the time, in a sitting with
the British medium Douglas Johnson, when his trance
personality, Chiang, a venerable Chinese sage, comment-
ing on the moral peccadilloes of mediums, with lofty off-
handedness said: "One is not too concerned over the
manners of a delivery boy, is one?")

But to return to psychic problems: Much of my pastoral
link with parapsychology has been in helping people who
have plunged into the occult and found themselves in
over their heads.

The most common cause or occasion of psychic problems is automatic writing. In this practice, which is tac-
itly encouraged by a number of popular books on the
market telling how the author by using it developed
wondrous psychic powers, the individual surrenders his
will to a pen. He, or more likely she, since more women
than men seem to take up automatic writing, holds the
pen loosely in her hand, lets her mind go blank, and
waits to receive something from the seventh astral plane.

At first the hand may simply twitch, then begin describing loops and whorls, almost as if the pen were getting
used to writing by itself, and finally script appears. The
script initially may be an illegible scrawl which, with
time and practice, becomes clearer until it can be read
as easily as the individual's normal handwriting.

And what does this writing—which the person truth-
fully insists comes "automatically," without any conscious
control—say and reveal?

The source usually is anonymous at first. The early
messages may take the form of vague, nice-nice spiritual
exhortations, sort of astral sermonizing. There may be
poetry (usually of deplorable quality). Often the autom-

atist (the person doing the automatic writing) is amazed because the script seems so different, in style, content, and appearance, from her normal handwriting. In some cases the script takes the form of mirror writing—that is, to be deciphered, it must be held up to a mirror. Or the words may be written backward.

Sooner or later, usually sooner, the purported author or authors of the writing get around to identifying themselves. Claiming usually to be spirits—though in this space age there are more and more extraterrestrials from Venus or some other planet—the author or authors promise to reveal to the automatist secrets hidden from the wise.

If to begin with there are several alleged communicators, these eventually are subsumed, as a rule, into a single communicator, who may continue to pass on messages from the others or let them, at times, control the pen directly.

Generally, it is not too long before the trouble starts (or, one might say, before it becomes evident). The communicator's tone subtly changes; he becomes dominating, then domineering. There may be threats, first veiled, then overt, that dire things will befall the automatist if the communicator's wishes are not carried out.

In many cases there are heavy sexual overtones, and these may become focused in outright obscenities. Lewd suggestions are made; unspeakable thoughts are propelled into the woman's mind (if it is a woman, and in such cases it usually is). She comes to feel that she is being taken over, possessed, by someone or something.

Sometimes the problem escalates, and the communicator manifests even when the individual is not doing automatic writing. She may begin to hear his voice, taunting her, threatening, making indecent suggestions, refusing to let her sleep. At this stage the victim may be a candidate for admission to a psychiatric hospital.

Psychic or Psychotic?

In such cases, what is really going on?

To the psychiatrist, it's fairly straightforward: The victim is suffering from acute neurosis, borderline psychosis, or even, depending on the severity of the symptoms, outright schizophrenia. The automatic writing emanates from her own unconscious mind; the voice or voices she hears are simply the auditory hallucinations common among schizophrenics.

The wise pastoral counselor listens carefully to the psychiatrist's viewpoint, recognizing that some of what passes for psychic experience is really psychotic. He appreciates that many of the people he sees who think they are being victimized by spirits are clearly victims of their own hallucinations and need psychiatric treatment, not exorcism. In fact, the informed pastoral counselor rarely, if ever, takes an alleged psychic experience absolutely at face value.

What do you say, for example, to a woman who comes to you, as one did to me, with the news that she has received a message from God by automatic writing that is so secret only you can know its content?

"Why me?" I asked.

"Because," she said breathlessly, "the message is that God has picked you to be the next Pope."

When I told the lady that, honored as I was, I might have to decline the office if it were offered to me, she looked at me for a moment, then left. Later she returned to inform me that God had changed his mind about me.

Another woman, who took up automatic writing after reading a book by Ruth Montgomery and then purchasing an "ESP pendulum" game by the mentalist Kreskin, came to me expecting to have her psychic experiences confirmed in the face of skepticism from her husband and others. She assured me that she had known Edgar Cayce in a previous life and was getting the language of the lost continent of Atlantis. She also informed me that in a former life I had been Joseph, the interpreter of dreams.

When I expressed skepticism, though as gently as possible, the woman's attitude toward me perceptibly changed. So did the automatic writing's. On the next visit she told me that in a previous life I also had been Doubting Thomas!

In this case it was especially difficult to reason the woman out of her fantasies because she seemed convinced that they were of God. She was, in fact, a devout Christian, which made the affliction even sadder. Faith that becomes deranged may be worse than no faith.

Sometimes, in order simply to keep my own sanity, I've had to stand back and laugh at what is happening. Such as the time a woman phoned me long distance and said: "I have a group of spirits—people who talk to me. I want to get rid of two of them."

"Why get rid of just two spirits?" I asked, somewhat surprised by this novel touch.

"Well," she explained, "the ones that like me come and go, but those that don't like me stay, and these two have to go!"

A psychic, she confided, had told her that one spirit would be gone by Christmas, but she wondered if I could speed things up a bit.

Professional mediums, of course, get more than their share of strange people. One prospective client told Chicago psychic Irene Hughes he wanted to know who he was going to be in his next life so that he could leave all his money to himself!

One of the unintentionally most hilarious cases was the man who confided to me that he slept with his dead wife every night—astrally, of course. She just climbed into bed with him in her spirit body, he said. He mentioned, too, that he received communications from the Virgin Mary; Joseph, the father of Jesus; St. John, and several others of similar status.

A married couple let me in on the news that they were getting regular messages from the late President Kennedy and had copies printed to send to their friends. Once when I sent them a book, I received in return a thank-you note signed "Jack Kennedy."

Emotional disturbance? Mental illness?

Yes, there is plenty of evidence of it in some people who dabble in the psychic. Of course, they might have become unbalanced on any subject with which they were emotionally involved; there are religious fanatics and political screwballs as well as psychic nuts. But, no doubt about it, the area of psychic experience does offer a rich and fertile soil for the growth of unhealthy fantasies of a peculiarly florid sort and outright delusional ideas.

Since the death of Arthur Ford, I have been inundated, not surprisingly, with messages purporting to be from him. Not one of these has been in the slightest convincing to me.

Much of the interest in getting communications from Ford was stimulated by the sales success of Ruth Montgomery's book *A World Beyond,* which purports to be based on messages Mrs. Montgomery received from Ford via automatic *typewriting* (it's faster than plain automatic writing, I guess).

"I had only to read Ruth Montgomery's book," effused one woman in a letter to me, "when this feeling arose like an undying tidal wave, and the words stood out on the page in *3D—Spiritual Frontiers Fellowship.*" This profound message, the lady was sure, had come from Arthur Ford.

Some of the communications from the late great medium are very friendly, even downright folksy, in a way that Arthur rarely if ever was in life.

"This is Art," one woman received by automatic writing. "You can call me in any time you please, morning, noon, or night. Just let me know beforehand, as I want to be certain that I'm available."

Another lady, who wanted to produce a book inspired by Ford just as Ruth Montgomery had, was admonished: "If we're going to work together you'll have to get a new ribbon in this typewriter!" Now, *that* sounds more like the real Arthur.

The Entanglement of Deep-Seated Emotional Conflicts

But besides fantasy and self-delusion in psychic problems, can something else be involved, something genuinely outside the person?

I believe that there can be, and sometimes is. And some psychiatrists, well informed in psychic matters, agree. Dr. Robert Laidlaw, a noted New York psychiatrist, spoke in my church about "possession" by discarnate spirits as a genuine possibility in some cases of mental illness and psychic derangement.

Many psychic problems are borderline; one hardly knows where the merely delusional ends and something else may begin. Consider such an ambiguous case from my experience.

A well-dressed, soft-spoken, good-looking woman of forty-three had developed an interest in psychic matters through her friendship with an older man, forty years her senior. She was impressed, she said, with this man's knowledge, gentleness, and his fatherlinesss toward her.

Before he died, he made a pact with the woman to communicate with her from the other side. This triggered a psychic mania. She became an incessant practitioner of automatic writing and soon was convinced that she was receiving messages from her deceased fatherly friend.

Typically, the messages at first were beautiful, religious. Later, however, their tone changed, and the woman developed an ambivalence toward the automatic writing—she still wanted to do it but, at the same time, she didn't. She was frightened by messages in which the old man said that he was in darkness, repeating this over and over.

She also worried about lies she discovered in the automatic script. She began to suspect that the old man, if it was he, was trying to gain her confidence by any means for some purpose of his own.

With each session of automatic writing the "power" became stronger, she said. Soon she felt a warmth in her hands, like an electric current. Her critical faculties—what was left of them—deserted her altogether, as when she expressed amazement that the automatic script told her exactly what she was wearing at the time!

Through the writing, the old man asked if she would allow him to put her into a trance, so that he could possess her. She said "Yes," but when she tried to let go and enter a trance, she felt a pain in her throat and roused with a start, realizing that she could die in the trance. Was this, she wondered, what the old man wanted?

At this point the woman sought help, and unfortunately didn't get it. She took her problem to her priest. He, presumably not informed in psychic matters, had no patience with her story and simply told her to see a psychiatrist.

Now the woman plunged deeper into the psychic maelstrom. Her sessions of automatic writing became even more frequent. But as the old man's spell over her grew stronger, something—her self-protective instinct, perhaps—made her increasingly fearful. Finally, in desperation, she came to me, not knowing really what she wanted except that it had to be something other than what she was then experiencing.

"The old man's with me all the time now," she said. "He's right here now. I don't have to do the writing any more; he just touches me on the arm. Spirit penetrates."

I am Freudian enough to have taken note of that last remark. What did her husband think of her psychic experiences? I asked.

"Oh, he considers it a very serious problem," she admitted.

I questioned her about her private life, if she had a close, loving relationship with her husband. She said, gravely, that there had been little intimacy during their years of marriage. She and her husband now slept in separate rooms, at least partly so that she could continue communing with the old man.

The old man, she confessed, had told her to change her hair style, to wear it in soft curls because he liked it that way. He helped her pick out a nightgown that pleased him. He instructed her to take a bath before going to bed.

"He won't leave me at night," she said, her voice trembling. "I am awakened by pounding on my shoulder. I have contractions in my stomach. I feel heat, cold, pain, and sweat, and *he* causes this!

"He's trying to get close to me. I wanted the love of a friend for a friend, but he wanted something different. I warned him, don't you come into my bedroom while my husband is there—you hear! He wanted—he wanted to experience love again."

Now we were approaching the heart of the matter.

Did she, I asked, consider sex a natural part of life?

At this, she broke down and sobbed.

"I'm not a physical person," she wept. "I don't enjoy life. I am an exile here. I'm not a real person. I love nature, not people."

"Do you have a family?" I asked.

"Yes," she said, "I have a son. He is twenty, but he has the soul of a woman—you see, my son was my mother in my last life."

I asked her if she went out in public much with her husband.

"I can't," she said. "I get a sense of this power when I'm with people. The old man can see people through me, taste through me, and hear through me. You see, he told me that in a former life I was a nun and he was a priest and we were lovers."

Clearly, sexual repression and hysteria were at the root of this woman's problems. Her deep-seated emotional conflicts provided a fertile soil for psychic fantasies, and the prospect was that there would be no easy, simple cure.

As I probed deeper, the woman revealed that when she was sixteen she had entered a convent and stayed for six years. The habits of sexual denial learned then, coupled with possibly too much teaching about sin, had created a warped psyche, an emotional blockage.

At my suggestion, the woman agreed to stop immediately automatic writing and all reading in the psychic field, and to see my friend the Reverend Roy Grace, a pastoral psychotherapist. With patience, and his expert help, I knew, she could be guided out of her labyrinth of tangled emotions and psychic delusions and restored to her husband as the warm, loving woman she was capable of being.

What Are the Remedies for Psychic Attack?

In psychic problem cases, the first step, as in this one, is to ban all activity related to the occult. This means no automatic writing, of course; no toying with the ouija board (which is simply another means by which the unconscious mind may be opened to—what?); no reading of psychic books nor listening to psychic lectures; nothing whatever even remotely pertaining to the psychic.

These measures may sound extreme, but they are necessary. A disturbed individual will never find the means to overcome his problem if it is constantly reinforced by his reading and thinking. Believe me, I have spent almost as much time arguing some people out of experimenting with the occult as arguing others into having an open mind about it.

There are some people, probably, who should stay away from the psychic completely, just as there are people who can't take a drink without becoming an alcoholic or a shot of a pain-killer without becoming an addict. Such people—few enough, fortunately—have innately unstable psychological constitutions, which make them prone to what I call "psychic attack."

By this phrase, I mean any phenomena such as we have been considering—delusions of spirit guidance, obsessive thoughts from spirits—as well as such manifestations as poltergeist eruptions. In these latter cases, the psychic attack is not purely subjective—inside the victim's mind—but takes place out there, in the external world, where everybody can see it. Objects fly around the room, icy breezes blow, doors slam shut, lights blink on and off—and withal, there is usually a definite, almost palpable sense of something sinister, threatening.

Most cases of psychic attack are triggered by the imprudent use of automatic writing and the ouija board. And in some cases heroic measures must be taken to stop the psychic assault. The most powerful weapons are prayer and the sacraments of the Church.

Hearing of Canon Robert Lewis's interest in psychic matters, a prominent Pennsylvania lawyer confided to him that his family was under psychic attack. The lawyer didn't call it that—he didn't know what to call it. But he didn't like what was happening.

There was a "cold spot" in a bedroom doorway at home where the temperature felt zero degrees year 'round, the lawyer said. The lights in the house went on and off erratically. Drapes on the window were seen to stick straight out, horizontally, as though blown by a strong wind, when the window was shut. Once, a teapot rose from a shelf and "floated" a few inches to another spot on the shelf.

The trouble started, the lawyer told Canon Lewis, after the family fooled with a ouija board on a Thanksgiving evening. They had sensed the presence of the lawyer's grandfather. Then something else seemed to take over, and the weird goings-on started and wouldn't stop.

In this case, contrary to the typical pattern, there were no adolescents in the home, only younger children.

On a first visit, Canon Lewis blessed the house, and the phenomena subsided. Later, however, they resumed. On a second visit, the Canon prepared holy water and performed the ancient rite of exorcism—the casting out of an evil spirit. Following this procedure, the phenomena ceased and have not returned.

The Perennial Controversy—Demonic Possession

This case, which involved exorcism, leads us to look at that controversial subject—demonic possession.

A wave of veritable demonomania swept the United States in the wake of the movie *The Exorcist*, which depicted the mysterious and terrifying experiences of a twelve-year-old girl possessed by the devil. The screenplay, and the book on which it was based, were said to be taken from an actual case of demon possession that occurred in 1951, in the Washington, D.C., area, involving a fourteen-year-old boy who was cured by exorcism.

Can demonic possession really occur?

This is a thorny question, depending a great deal on the definition of terms. And there is no unanimity about an answer, even in the Roman Catholic Church. Three Jesuits acted as technical advisers in the movie *The Exorcist*, attesting that the eerie happenings in the film were based on actual events, which they believed had been due to demonic possession.

However, another Jesuit priest, the Reverend Juan B. Cortes, professor of psychology at Georgetown University, where part of the movie was shot, said he does not believe in demonic possession in the sense in which the film does. "Demon," he suggests, is simply a prescientific word for what today we call a "complex," or an emotional conflict. The bizarre symptoms of demonic possession—throwing oneself about, uncontrollable cursing, violence, strange marks on the skin—can all be explained, says Father Cortes, as those of certain brain and nervous disorders.

My personal interpretation of demon possession is midway between the traditional view and that espoused by Father Cortes. The traditional view says that demons are evil intelligences or personalities *that have never had a physical body* and roam the Earth seeking victims to destroy. In support of this view many biblical passages can be cited, especially those from the Gospels in which Jesus cast out devils.

My partial dissent from this traditional view is over the issue of whether demons are really nonhuman intelligences, or whether what we call demons may actually be depraved human spirits. I do not deny that demons, in the traditional nonhuman sense, exist; I say simply that in my experience, and that of others, contemporary cases of genuine possession appear to involve the degenerate spirits of deceased human beings.

As a matter of faith, I accept the possibility of malignant nonhuman intelligences able to oppress people, confident that if such do exist they, too, are subject to the power of God; but in actual possession cases my psychic experiences lead me to regard depraved human spirits as the probable cause.

At the beginning of this book I described the eeriest experience of my life, the night when, in a house by the New Jersey coast, a hypnotized subject appeared to be possessed by an alien entity. That intruder acted like a lost, woeful human spirit rather than a traditional demon. The intruder, through the possessed woman's lips, cried out for the light. In the name of Christ, I bade the vagrant soul seek the light, and he did.

I believe too deeply in the reality of evil to take lightly the possibility of possession by someone or something with vile intentions toward man. The present craze for witchcraft and Satanism among young people disturbs me, for they are playing with fire that may burn far worse than most of them can imagine.

A Resurgence of Satanism

In California it is no longer uncommon for the police to pick up young people carrying ritual bags filled with implements for the celebration of the Black Mass, drugs, love potions, animal bones, and occasionally even human fingers. This is dabbling in darkness.

West Coast residents in isolated areas have complained of ritual chanting at night, and later have discovered skinned cats and beheaded chickens around what had been a ceremonial fire. Among Caribbean and black peoples of New York, voodoo and other rituals are openly advertised in the Spanish-language and underground press.

In the city of Vineland, New Jersey, not far from Wood-bury, where I live, two high school youths were arrested for assisting in the ritual murder of a teen-aged Satanist who insisted that he undergo a violent death in order to take over command of forty leagues of demons. Some ten years ago, another case of Satanist ritual murder occurred in the same city and, recalling the traditional attachment of witches' covens to a particular site, one is inclined to wonder about Vineland.

All this black magic, Satanism, witchcraft, voodoo, and other sick and sinister manifestations of a bizarre fascination with the occult, play into the hands of those religious critics who are only too quick to condemn anything psychic as of the devil. But we must not fall into that trap.

Sane, mature, spiritually minded explorers of the psychic world are no more to be equated with occult freaks and sickies than are most fundamentalists with the revivalist racketeers, the Marjoes and the A. A. Allen's, who bilk people of millions in the name of Jesus. It is as reprehensible to lump Christians whose faith has been enriched by their psychic experiences with black magicians as it would be to lump all evangelists with Bible-thumping religious racketeers.

The exploration of the psychic world is not without some risk, but is anything? It's risky getting out of bed in the morning, visiting new places, thinking new thoughts, seeking deeper experiences of God. But to stop taking spiritual risks is, virtually, to stop living spiritually.

Once, during a tooth extraction under a general anesthetic, I had a dramatic "vision" of my friend Eileen Garrett, the medium.

As I sank into the dark oblivion induced by the anesthetic, ahead of me was a pinpoint of light, which at my approach grew steadily larger and brighter until it was like the blaze of a thousand arc lamps. Merging into the light I heard, clearly, unmistakably, the voice of Eileen Garrett.

"This is what it's all about, Billy," she said in her familiar way, "all that we discussed. . . . Remember, the point of light is the point of trust."

The experience was so real and powerful that I had a small diamond put into the cross I often wear—the diamond to represent that "point of light" that is "the point of trust." Whenever I look at a gem, quivering in the light, or see the sun's rays rainbowing through a stained-glass window, I think of those words of Eileen Garrett.

The point of light and trust is Christ. Keep your eyes on Him, and your psychic experiences will be beautiful and fulfilling.

11

REINCARNATION
Have We Lived Before?

My position on reincarnation is simply this: I do not affirm it as a matter of faith, nor do I deny it as a matter of possibility.

Within the limits of this statement there is ample room to investigate, probe, weigh facts, and speculate about the puzzling question: Have we lived before?

There is some evidence that points toward a positive answer to the question, and I've had some experiences that tend to suggest reincarnation. However, since I'm writing this book as a priest as well as a psychic investigator, I must take note of what Christian tradition and teaching have to say about reincarnation.

Surprisingly, to some people perhaps, Dr. Leslie Weatherhead, the noted minister-psychologist, former pastor of London's historic City Temple and former president of the Methodist Conference of Great Britain, believes in reincarnation. He has defended that belief, as a Christian, in his booklet *The Case for Reincarnation*, and he devoted a chapter to it in his larger book *The Christian Agnostic*.

Dr. Weatherhead argues that not only is Church teaching and tradition ambiguous on the subject of reincarnation (at least one of the great Church Fathers, Origen, profoundly believed in the doctrine), but the New Testament is not so plainly antireincarnation as some very orthodox scholars would have us think.

Weatherhead cites a number of references in the Gospel that he says can plausibly be interpreted as at least suggesting reincarnation. Indeed, he argues that what these passages show is that in Jesus' day the idea of reincarnation was not something alien and outlandish but almost taken for granted.

Weatherhead uses a familiar passage in the ninth chapter of St. John's Gospel, which has been quoted against reincarnation, as a proreincarnation argument. The story tells how a man *born* blind was brought to Jesus with the question: "Master, who did sin, this man or his parents, that he was born blind?" Now, leaving aside for the moment Jesus' answer, Weatherhead argues that the question seems to imply quite clearly a belief in reincarnation; otherwise it's hard to see how it could have made any sense: "Master . . . [did this man sin] . . . that he was born blind?" Obviously, any sin the man had committed must have been in a previous life.

Weatherhead cites this, I repeat, not to show Jesus' approval or disapproval of reincarnation (Jesus said in this case that neither the man or his parents had sinned), but to show the currency of the idea at that time. Also, Weatherhead notes, Jesus did not say in his reply: "Your question is absurd," as we might have expected if reincarnation were all nonsense.

There are several other passages Weatherhead quotes—Jesus referring to John the Baptist as Elijah who was to come again; and the disciples' remarks, in answer to one of Jesus' questions, that many said he was Jeremiah, Elijah, "or one of the prophets," meaning, presumably, a reincarnation of one of them—but these, and Weatherhead's entire argument, can be read in his books.

Psychic Investigations with Savonarola

My interest in this chapter is to look at reincarnation from the standpoint primarily of the psychic investigator; to offer some evidence from my own experience, which seems to point to reincarnation; but ultimately to leave the question open as one unnecessary to salvation, though fascinating to think about.

There is a curious sequence of events involving myself and a purported link with the famous Florentine monk and reformer Savonarola.

At a sitting with Arthur Ford, Fletcher, his spirit guide, said, that in a former life I was "a disciple of Savonarola" and that with other of his followers I had been banished from Florence. (Savonarola, a Dominican, had a terrible feud with Alexander VI, the Borgia Pope, and was finally sentenced to death with two companions and hanged (and later burned) in Florence's public square, the Piazza della Signaria, in 1498. He was charged with heresy, but his real offense was his outspoken opposition to the abuses of the papal court.)

Just before I left my first parish in Florence, New Jersey, to become rector of Christ Church, Woodbury, I visited the then rector, the Reverend Canon Robert G. W. Williams, and his wife. After looking at me for a few moments, Mrs. Williams said: "We have a lot of things to dispose of. I have two pictures—do you want them? I'll show them to you."

I looked at the pictures. One was an interpretation of a scene from Joshua's life and didn't interest me. But the other—well, the other was a print of what appeared to be a cloister, a monastery. I looked at it for a moment, wondering if I had seen it before, though I felt sure I hadn't.

"What is this?" I asked Mrs. Williams.

"Oh, this," she said, wiping away the dust on it. "We've had this for a long time. This is the tomb of Savonarola."

Coincidence? That after Fletcher told me of a link with Savonarola I should encounter a picture linked to him in this curious way? Well, I have visited many—what, dozens, scores of?—rectories in my time, but never have I seen another picture, nor heard of one, called "The Tomb of Savonarola." Actually, I discovered the framed print depicted the cloister of San Marco in Florence, where Savonarola once lived with his fellow monks.

Savonarola faded from my thoughts, though the curious coincidence of the picture impressed me, I admit. I hung the picture in my room.

Then, some while later, I had a sitting in London with Douglas Johnson, a medium then on the staff of the College of Psychic Studies. Johnson did psychometry. Holding a personal object of mine in his hands, he picked up images from my present and past: the new house my parents were building in Highlands, New Jersey; the river I knew as a boy, and the boats sailing on it. Then he asked me if I were going to Italy.

"You have," he said, "a very strong pull to Italy."

Well, I did go to Italy, to Florence, where I visited the monastery of San Marco. It would be colorful to be able to report that I had a dramatic *déjà vu* experience, that scenes from my life with Savonarola and the monks rushed before my eyes, that the past became alive. But it didn't. Actually, I felt a profound serenity, a sense of belonging, but nothing more. Yet, as I think of it now, there was about that monastery an encompassing aura of wellbeing, peace, and contentment such as I have not felt often in strange places. Was it, perhaps, because it wasn't strange?

There was a moment of special tranquillity when I stood in one of the deserted halls of the monastery, which I imagined echoing to the shuffling feet of the monks, and gazed at the preaching chair Savonarola used. I felt peace there.

Some months later, when I had returned to my parish, I visited a lady who had expressed an interest in psychic matters. During our conversation she told me how an appreciation of the mystical life had reawakened her interest in the New Testament. Then, as I was on my way out, I noticed in the hallway a chair that seemed familiar. It looked like Savonarola's, the one I had seen in the monastery of San Marco.

When I remarked on the chair, the woman said: "You may have it. Please take it. I've been thinking of giving it to you."

The chair is almost a duplicate of Savonarola's and contains in the backpiece a profile of the fiery monk in ivory. Brought from Florence in the 1930s, it now stands in the rectory in Woodbury. And when I look at it, something stirs in me.

But I wasn't through with Savonarola. A few weeks later the phone rang and a parishioner asked me if I wanted a picture she owned, an etching, Raphael's "Disputation of the Sacrament." Since only two copies of this etching were in existence, she said, she wanted to give one to the church.

She began describing the picture, and when she remarked that Savonarola was in it, I asked why she specifically mentioned him. She said: "No reason." The name was the only one she remembered from the list she once saw of the code of the picture.

Then, some time after accepting this etching for the church, a small, hand-painted dish also came into my possession. On it was a portrait of the great heretic of Florence.

So a picture, a chair, an etching, and a painted dish, all bearing the image or stamp of Savonaraola, have dropped into my life since Fletcher told me: "You were one of his disciples." Meaningful coincidence? Or something more?

"Reflections in the Mirror of the Mind"

Other lives, I know, have been touched by the possibility of reincarnation—the possibility that, deep within us, we carry what one medium called "reflections in the mirror of the mind" of experiences we have lived in time and space but not in this present life.

In my parish the Yeiter family recalls with seriousness the frequent remarks of their son that he "remembered" a previous time before this life.

Sherman was only five and one half years old at the time, but was able to express himself with a skill beyond his years. Apparently since starting to talk, he had mentioned to his family that he could remember having been here before.

Sometimes when they were on a trip, the lad would say: "I've been over this bridge before," or "I walked through this house before."

The parents used to immediately correct him, explaining that he couldn't possibly have been there because this was his first visit, but the boy would reply: "Oh, I don't mean with you. Before I came to you, to this family."

Once he said, out of the blue: "I was with my other family before I came to you."

Apart from this quirk, if that's what it was, the child wasn't particularly imaginative and didn't go in for spinning tall stories. Finally, the very matter-of-factness with which he spoke about his "other family" made his parents wonder if there could be something more to it than a childish fantasy.

Can Past Lives Affect Present Ones?

A child in my parish, Karen Shields, then three years old, startled her mother when, during a bedtime story in which someone died, Karen suddenly said: "No one ever dies, Mummy. Every time a baby's born it's somebody coming back."

This, from a three-year-old, took her mother aback. And when the child was nine, and her grandmother died, she said to her mother gravely: "Now I know what that word is—reincarnation. Remember when I told you? I still believe that."

Gary Civalier, brother of an Episcopal priest friend, startled his family with what seemed to be memories of a previous life. Episodes that appeared to be flashbacks to an earlier period of history started when the boy was only three (this age seems to be significant in such cases). He said he remembered his life in the Old West during the era of wagon trains, frontier towns, and Indian raids.

Imagination? The influence of television?

The boy's parents didn't think so. His claimed memories seemed far too vivid, rich, and detailed for that.

"You don't need to tell me about it—I know," the boy said impatiently to his parents who attempted to describe pioneer life as the history books report it.

"How do you know?" the parents asked, not mocking but with evident sincerity.

"I was there," the boy said with equally evident sincerity.

The boy, now in his twenties, still has his uncanny sense of identification with the Old West. It happens that his forebears, on his father's side, were among the original settlers of Arizona and homesteaded there, but at three years of age, when his prior-life "fantasies" started, the boy did not know that. Today, he feels a magnetic pull to the West.

Such cases prove nothing, of course, but they do make one wonder. . . .

Sometimes mediums who know nothing about a person are able to account for certain of his predilections in this life in terms of influences from a previous life. In fact, according to what some mediums have revealed, we carry around within us interests, inclinations, and aptitudes— and no doubt weaknesses and vestigial vices—brought from former Earth lives.

Once I took to see Arthur Ford a man who was puzzled, quite genuinely puzzled, by his own sudden, overpowering thirst for knowledge about ancient Egypt. His Egyptological curiosity had become a passion; more, almost a craze. He was haunting museums, spending a small fortune on books and pictures about Egypt, and even developed an urge to take photographs of the sun —something that struck him as really weird and, in terms of his previous experiences, totally out of character for him.

Ford, who had no knowledge of the sitter nor of his Egyptological obsession, no sooner went into trance than Fletcher began bringing through a veritable stream of names from the world of archaeology. Then he did what was fairly uncommon in Ford's mediumship: He gave a "life reading" of the man, linking the present situation to his previous incarnations. His interest in Egypt, said Fletcher, was a karmic pattern—"karmic" meaning a reaping now of what was sown before.

Fletcher said: "Someone comes named Humboldt. He was a German scholar. He's attracted to you because he wants to tell you something. He's coming because of something in your mind, and he wants to explain why that something *is* in your mind.

"Make a note of this: Arthur Weigall. He says he was one of those who died because of an ancient curse about disturbing a tomb. Humboldt tells me that the ancient Egyptians, when they mummified their kings, if they did not want the tomb to be disturbed, very cleverly mixed and painted onto some of the sacred mummies a very potent poison.

"Anybody handling these objects, especially if they took them into a bright light, into the sunlight, absorbed the poison through their skins. He thinks that's the reason so many died who excavated the tombs of the ancient kings. Magic to the ignorant; poison to the intelligent. In either case, it worked, and it worked on me."

At this point, the deceased archaeologist, Weigall, apparently had elbowed Humboldt aside and was communicating through Ford directly.

"I was one of five," he went on, "and I was an Englishman. What I can gather from this wave of consciousness that comes floating from you [the sitter] is that at some point in your previous lifetimes you were . . . Thotmes . . . and there's a three after it . . . Thotmes three . . . Thotmes the Third. . . ."

On another occasion Ford gave a life reading to a very disturbed young man who had a domineering father with whom he was in constant conflict. As a result, the young man was withdrawing more and more into himself. I had tried to help him by pastoral counseling, but his deep, violent resentment toward his father seemed to block any change for the better in his general attitudes.

Again, Ford knew nothing about the sitter or his circumstances. But he went into a very deep trance (his trances varied in depth; as a frequent observer, I could tell this quite accurately, I think), and Fletcher described a karmic condition from a past life. These revelations led to remarkable changes in the boy's attitudes toward himself, his father, and the world at large.

In three trance sittings, Fletcher perceived the whole family situation and described it explicitly. The discarnates who, as I believe, spoke through him set the young man straight in his thinking at a very critical period in his life.

"When I look at him," Fletcher said of this young man, "I see someone very old, very old. He has been here before, this one."

Some excerpts from Ford's trance utterances on those occasions show how he was able to give guidance to the sitter.

"You chose to be where you are now, in this life, because you were very cruel to someone, I think the one who is now your father, and in your own person you had to receive that same cruelty.

"In the small village of Cappula, in what is now Italy, you were only thirty-three when you died. You were very ruthless, but you were the product of your time. You have fulfilled your obligation; you have suffered in this life humiliation, as you caused it to others in that earlier life.

"I see you lying on the floor with your face down and your arms and hands outstretched, crying. You have done that?"

The sitter said "Yes."

"But this is a scene—that is, a reproduction of a scene —that occurred in the fifteenth century; yes, about the fifteenth century in Cappula or Capua.

"You were then the dominant one and someone else cried, someone else wondered why you beat him rather than let him serve you. And in this life you had to experience that—but it is finished now.

"When a karmic problem is in the process of being solved, it becomes acute. And unless the person understands what is going on, it is a very confusing and frustrating time.

"Know this: You chose to be born who you are; your parents simply provided the physical vehicle. And because at some past time you were in a position of authority where you were able to hurt someone in a very cruel manner, someone in this life has hurt you. That someone was a slave, then. And the moral and ethical standards of that time did not oblige you to show consideration for a slave. Now he is dominant and shows no consideration for you. You earned it; you asked for a chance to pay off this karmic debt in this life, and you got the chance.

"Now you've paid the debt. You've allowed this one whom you hurt to hurt you. But you cannot live your entire life being hurt. There comes a time when you must experience the resurrection. The ego dies, the *I*, and with it all its unconscious memories must be buried. And you must be resurrected into a new life, a life of love. It isn't easy, and it won't be easy for you.

"I want you, the next time you kneel at the altar to take Communion, to say to yourself what your Lord said, 'I paid the price, even unto death I paid the price. Now I am free to become one of those who help others to be free.'"

Fletcher's insights and counsel changed that young man's life, so much so that at a later sitting Ford, in trance, said: "You have made great progress since you were here before. Someone here in spirit is telling me that. You are learning that love casts out hate."

At a still later sitting, Fletcher assessed the young man's emotional and spiritual health by reading his aura (the aura is the emanation of light, said to surround each one of us, that serves as a barometer of our thoughts and feelings).

"When I look at your aura," Fletcher said to the young man, "it tells me a great deal about your emotional and mental or spiritual—and even physical—condition. The signs are still there that you have been through a severe emotional upheaval. There are a lot of yellow and deep orange shades in the aura, which indicate anger and fighting, not on a physical but an emotional basis. These shades are like arrows, like streaks, which penetrate the basic blue of the aura. The blue represents your fundamental nature, which is mental and spiritual."

Reincarnation and God

What about reincarnation as a principle? Is everybody subject to a law of rebirth?

"Reincarnation," Fletcher said to me once, "is a law for those who believe it. But Jesus came to fulfill the law, the law of an eye for an eye and a tooth for a tooth. Jesus didn't destroy, He fulfilled. And now, He said, you are no longer subject to the law, you are under Grace.

"In other words, when you have grace you have free will. Grace means simply free will, and time, and a second chance; that's what it really means. So you can choose.

"Now, Jesus *chose* to incarnate in order that He might share His knowledge with people of His own faith, a people who, as a nation, had a lot of laws, rules, and traditions. Great souls do reincarnate, but they don't have to.

"You can choose. And that's one reason why I—Fletcher talking now—why I'm doing this job through Ford. By doing it through him I'm balancing the account.

"I wasn't a very good person, you see, in my Earth life, I did some pretty nasty things. And so I'm trying to put enough good into circulation that I'll never have to get involved again.

"When Ford conks out and comes over here, I'll be free. I won't work for anyone then and I can go on. Well, thank you for all you have done for my instrument. I'm very glad that you have been his friend."

Fletcher, I trust, has found now that freedom of which he spoke; he's at liberty to "go on," and I wish him Godspeed.

Reincarnation?

The important truth, it seems to me, is that whether or not reincarnation is a "law," there is another superior to it, by which its action can be transcended, annulled, set aside; and that is the law of grace.

"The law of grace hath made us free from the law of sin and death."

And, if it exists, rebirth . . .

EPILOGUE
The New Is Old

The Church must learn, in relation to the psychic world, the profound meaning of St. Augustine's words:

> The new in the old concealed,
> The old in the new revealed.

There is nothing new about visions, telepathy, healings, clairvoyance, prophecy, and similar manifestations, and yet the Church too long has neglected such subjects.

Time was when men were awed by the miracles of Christ. But then came the scientist in his white coat, with his test tubes and calipers, and mystery was banished and miracles were forbidden to exist.

After a brief skirmish, the Church as a whole accepted the new rationalist dogma quietly enough, almost meekly. Instead of trying to reinterpret miracles as higher expressions of nature's laws, the Church, with unseemly haste, renounced them as embarrassing, almost scandalous contradictions of those laws. Miracles, it was decided, were simply perfectly ordinary events misperceived by the myopic eye of faith.

But as England's Rev. G. Maurice Elliott, long-time secretary of the Churches' Fellowship for Psychical and Spiritual Studies, said: "Yesterday's miracles are today's natural laws." That was in his book *The Psychic Life of Jesus,* in which Elliott, an Anglican priest, reconceptualized the miracles of Christ in the light of the profounder understanding of nature revealed by psychic research.

Today, with the growth of parapsychology and the occult explosion, the pressure is greater than it was in Elliott's time for a reinterpretation of Christian faith in the light of our knowledge of man's psychic nature. In a world where psychokinesis can happen, for example, the old objections to Jesus walking on the water lose their force. Of course, what He did was not "normal," but "supernormal." It was, however, natural, in the fullest sense of that word.

Parapsychology shows that nature has laws that we have not yet grasped. Jesus, as a master of the spirit, understood these intuitively, as a musical genius does harmony or a master painter does form and color. What Jesus used to perform His miracles was the "higher magic" in which nature's hidden laws are manipulated by those who understand them.

Mind you, I am not suggesting that prayer is only telepathy, or that prophecy, in the biblical sense, is merely precognition. Otherwise one could find himself arguing that God were simply a sort of superghost! In this book I have taken considerable pains to refute the notion that psychic and spiritual realities are identical. However, they do overlap, as the experiences I have reported make abundantly plain, and each can help us to a more complete understanding of the other.

As a priest, my faith, I repeat, is not based on psychic phenomena; however, such phenomena support, strengthen, and inform that faith.

Even the negative aspects of the psychic world confirm my Christian philosophy. Believing in the reality of evil as a force opposing God, I am not in the least surprised to find that force manifesting in psychic experiences, as in every other area of human behavior, from business and sex to politics and religion. Where there is faith there must also be at least the possibility of doubt. Similarly, if a psychic energy exists that can increase the growth of living things, a Christian theologian would expect some inversion of that force also to exist. This is simply another expression of what modern theologians call the demonic—the disintegrative, nihilistic aspect of reality that stands over against the creative power of God.

Let me put it this way: In a world where love can make alive, hate can kill. And where it is possible to bless, it must also be possible to curse.

With mediums, as with other human beings, one would expect to find the good and the bad, the sincere and the spurious, the dedicated and the cynical, those who use their gifts wisely and humanely and those who misuse or abuse them.

Many aspects of Christian faith and practice for me have taken on a new and tingling reality as a result of my psychic investigations—for example, the power of prayer. Prayer, I see now, is essentially directed thought (in the old hymn, "the heart's sincere desire"). And thought is energy transmitted by the mind. This thought energy is almost electric in its comings and goings.

Though I would not go so far as a distinguished Roman Catholic theologian, the Reverend Arthur Gibson, who said "the soul is an electronic event," I do find great meaning in the concept of man's spiritual energies as a force akin to electricity that can run down and be recharged, that flows, and that produces real results.

Prayer, I realize too, is a skill—a knack, if you like—that must be exercised in order to be developed. People *can* learn to pray. They can learn how to generate prayer power.

My psychic research has fortified my conviction that prayer should be used for the sick, for those who mourn, for all in need, and for those who have shed their physical bodies and entered postgraduate studies in the school of life.

All prayer probably involves telepathic communication. This makes it more real to me. With a solid conviction based on the empirical data of parapsychology, I know that in prayer, as in telepathy, there is no distance. The one for whom I pray, or who prays for me, is somehow joined with me, though an ocean may separate us. When we say, "keep a place for me in your prayers," as "keep a place for me in your thoughts," we're speaking of a place which, though it has no latitude or longitude, is nonetheless real for that.

Distance, I've come to believe, is spiritual, not physical. People who are one in spirit or telepathic rapport *are* one, though thousands of miles stretch between them. And those who are spiritually estranged are distant, though they sit side by side. My psychic explorations make these things literal facts for me and not mere pious sentiments.

Similarly, the "communion of saints" is for me no prayer book cliché but something quite as real as the NBC Television Network. In this mysterious, psychic universe all of us are bound to each other by invisible threads.

Parapsychology is not an enemy of faith but the best friend faith has. I am inclined to agree with Dr. J. B. Rhine, the father of statistical studies of ESP, who reiterated to me his dictum that parapsychology is religion's basic science.

"What physics is to engineering and biology is to medicine," he said, "parapsychology is to religion."

One important expression of the psychic renaissance is the growth of Church-oriented groups dedicated to creating a rapprochement between mainstream religion and paranormal experience. Such a group is Spiritual Frontiers Fellowship, which can be recommended as a trustworthy source of guidance for seekers trying to find their way in the sometimes treacherous terrain of the psychic world.

The history of SFF, in which I've played a small but for me very meaningful part, is instructive because it serves as another measure of how Church interest in the psychic over the past two decades has mushroomed.

Spiritual Frontiers Fellowship began in March 1956, when a Methodist clergyman, Paul Lambourne Higgins; a Disciples of Christ educator and missionary, now deceased, Albin Bro; and the amazing Arthur Ford met in Chicago to discuss the formation of a group that would help to restore to the Churches an awareness of their psychical and mystical heritage. Another meeting was called in Chicago and a program planned.

The letter that was sent to announce that historic first meeting reflects what the founders envisioned.

> Dear Friends:
> Some of us have felt it upon our hearts to plan a seminar of spiritual and psychical studies looking toward the organization of a group devoted to the exploration of the frontiers of the spirit. England's Churches' Fellowship for Psychical Studies is serving a real need. A group with similar motives is needed in America.
> You are among a limited number of persons being invited to a Spiritual Frontiers Fellowship seminar to be held March 4–5, 1956, in the Hyde Park Methodist Church, Chicago. . . .

Even then, some twenty years ago, those SFF founders detected a rising tide of interest in the Churches in psychic phenomena, especially in relation to prayer, healing, and life after death. They felt that if these areas of experience continued to be neglected, the Churches' spiritual vitality would wither.

In 1957, a year after SFF's founding, Arthur Ford sent me a notice that he was to speak at an SFF-sponsored seminar in Trenton, New Jersey, in the Presbyterian church. The pastor, the Reverend Monroe Drew, was a brave man who in those days was really bucking the religious tide. I attended that SFF seminar, one of a relative handful of ecclesiastical eccentrics willing to admit an interest in such spooky stuff, and I haven't lost interest in SFF since. Eventually, from 1964 to 1968, I served two terms as its president.

Today SFF is an international organization, with almost ten thousand members in all states (and in Puerto Rico, Canada, and England). From the seventy-five who attended that first conference, the number has risen to two thousand (the conferences are still held in Chicago).

Members of all denominations, from Roman Catholicism to Unitarianism, both clergy and laity, are in SFF. What has attracted them?

Well, that of course is in large part what this book is about. New SFFers are seeking something that they have not found in their Church. They want a deeper and broader grasp of life's meaning for themselves. They want a more vital and pulsating religious experience. They seek truths to stretch the mind, far horizons to lure them on, depths in which they can take soundings on the ultimate questions of life, death, and after.

SFF has a distinctive identity in the psychic world. Unlike professional parapsychologists, it is not content merely to study ESP from a purely scientific and secular perspective. Its viewpoint is frankly religious. It asks: What does this or that psychic phenomenon, attested by science, *mean* for religious values and experience? How does it deepen our understanding of man and God? And unlike religious fringe groups, SFF is not in business to compete with the Churches—precisely the opposite. Its *raison d'être* is to strengthen the Church.

As parapsychological research accelerates, new data

will create new questions for the Church. SFF exists to show how such questions can be answered.

More and more, man will question his familiar concepts of time because of the profound paradox of precognition, which makes a mockery of past, present, and future. More and more, he will question his concepts of space, which is demolished by telepathy and clairvoyance. More and more, he will question traditional notions of life after death that do not stand up under psychical scrutiny.

In view of the emergence of the "occulture," SFF's credo is more timely today than when it was espoused nearly two decades ago: "This is Spiritual Frontiers Fellowship, called by God, we believe, for such a time as this. . . ."

The more I penetrate into the mysteries of the psychic world, the more I learn about ESP, psychokinesis, out-of-the-body states, and astral travel, the more I realize what I always knew: In, around, under, and over the material universe there broods an ineffable perfect Thinker; a sublime Artist seeking to perfect a flawed masterpiece; a supreme Architect building from atoms the whirling galaxies; a cosmic Musician weaving harmonies beautiful enough to make up for all the sorrows of the world.

My faith and my psychic experiences alike tell me that everything has purpose. Not a tear is wasted, not a cup of water given in vain. All experience is part of some great whole. All rivers flow toward one immortal sea. All paths lead irresistibly at last to one great homecoming.

And the name of all this wonder is God, whom Jesus taught us to call "Father." . . .

APPENDIX I
The Houdini Mystery Solved

Did Arthur Ford really contact the spirit of Houdini?

Did Ford psychically reveal the coded message said to be known only to the late great magician and his wife?

And did Ford thereby convince Houdini's widow, Beatrice, that truly she had communicated with her dead husband?

The mystery of the Houdini code message has resisted attempts at solution since it sprouted, on the front pages, back in 1929. Headlines across the United States shouted that Arthur Ford, the medium, had spoken the message agreed upon between Houdini and his wife before his death. Editorials were written about the episode. Magicians and mediums traded insults about it. Psychic researchers argued about it. And a great many people wondered about it.

But when the furor had subsided (though it continues to smolder right up to the present), nobody seemed to know the truth of the matter.

During my psychic investigations, I came across evidence (by mere coincidence or by some hidden design, depending upon your interpretation) that sheds a new and startling light on the mystery of the Houdini code message. Now, after more than forty years, it is possible to solve the mystery, if not with absolute certainty, then with a degree of probability so high as to be virtually conclusive.

The evidence I have uncovered indicates that Arthur Ford gained his knowledge of the Houdini message by devious means. The story of exactly how he did it, and in so doing creating one of the legends of the psychic world, is as wild and zany as were the Roaring Twenties themselves.

It is necessary to summarize the events leading up to the Houdini message. (For the full story, see the chapter "The Houdini Affair" in *Arthur Ford: The Man Who Talked with the Dead*.)

When Harry Houdini, the greatest magician and escapologist of his time, died on October 31, 1926, he was said to have left his wife a message, known only to the two of them, which he would attempt to communicate from the other side as proof of his survival. The message was "Rosabelle believe," and the second word was to be communicated in the code the Houdinis had used in a mind-reading act years before.

Houdini had a reputation as a ghost-buster. He was the scourge of fake mediums, and his crusade against them paid off not only in mediums exposed and in many cases convicted of fraud in court, but in the form of booming box-office receipts as well. For Houdini, scourging phony mediums was profitable as well as pious.

Houdini had an edge on the fake mediums because he had been one of them and knew their tricks. In his twenties, when he traveled with a "spook show," he used to comb cemeteries looking for information for his mediumistic messages. But Houdini, for all his skepticism, had a more than sneaking suspicion that there was something to this talking-to-the-dead business. His superstitions were of Transylvanian proportions. He was quick to interpret any unusual incident as a "sign" that someone was trying to contact him from the beyond, and he generally seemed anything but the cold-blooded realist that some of his more uncritical admirers have made him out to be.

The final evidence that he was no real skeptic is the deathbed covenant Houdini made with his wife—to contact her from the grave.

In the two years after his death, Mrs. Houdini—who originally offered a ten-thousand-dollar reward for the correct message but then withdrew it—was deluged by spirit messages of every description. Most of them belonged to the nut category. Mrs. Houdini said many of the writers gave every evidence of being "insane." None of the messages contained the secret words.

Then, in January 1928, Arthur Ford, the dapper, debonair pastor of New York's First Spiritualist Church, announced that through his spirit guide, Fletcher, he had received a message purporting to come from Houdini's mother. The message consisted of the single word:

FORGIVE.

"Houdini's widow" Bess (as her friends called her) was excited. FORGIVE, she allowed, was the word that Houdini had hoped to hear from mediums after his mother's death. If he had received it in his lifetime, she said, he would have accepted spirit communication.

However, the evidentiality of this message was considerably weakened by the disclosure that some time before, Mrs. Houdini herself had mentioned the key word in an interview with the Brooklyn *Eagle* (March 13, 1927) which she apparently had forgotten.

Then, in a series of sittings, Arthur Ford received what was said to be the message Houdini had left with his wife. Emissaries were sent to her to report that the first word of the message was "Rosabelle." If she acknowledged this, said Ford, she was to attend a séance at which the remainder of the message would be communicated in code, and deciphered.

Beatrice Houdini, in bed recovering from a fall when Ford's emissaries arrived, reportedly greeted their news with the exclamation: "My God! What else did he say?"

The word "Rosabelle," she acknowledged, was the first part of the secret message. Could the medium produce the rest of it? Of course she agreed to a séance, to be held at her home.

That dramatic event took place on January 7, 1929. During the séance Ford, purportedly in trance, gave a series of words, explained that they were part of the code the Houdinis had used onstage years before, then deciphered them as the single word: BELIEVE.

The entire message, therefore, was: ROSABELLE BELIEVE.

Beatrice Houdini affirmed that this message was correct in every particular and signed a notarized statement to that effect. The story hit the papers the same day—and boom! Controversy exploded.

Ford was accused of fraud, and so was Mrs. Houdini. They were both in it together, said some, as a publicity stunt. Not so, countered others; Mrs. Houdini was a dear, sweet lady who had been hoodwinked by the big, bad medium.

Magicians jumped into the fray, pointing out that the Houdini mind-reading code was no secret anyway, since it had been published in 1928 in a biography of Houdini by Kellock on page 105.

The New York *Graphic,* perhaps the yellowest of all tabloids in the United States, screamed in headlines a mile high that the Houdini message was a hoax that Ford and the magician's widow had cooked up together to make money. Mrs. Houdini tearfully denied it; Ford called the *Graphic* story a tissue of lies.

And so the debate raged. The Spiritualists defended their hero to the hilt (except for a brief interlude in which an anti-Ford faction tried to depose him from his pastorate). Arthur Ford was a genius and a saint, went the Spiritualists' litany; he was the greatest medium since the Fox sisters, maybe greater. The magicians just as fiercely derided him as a trickster, a phony; in other words, one of themselves.

The story was clouded even more when Mrs. Houdini, after initially defending her own sincerity, and Ford's, in vigorous terms, seemed to have second thoughts. Eventually she came to flatly deny that she had ever received a communication from her husband. However, there was the little matter of her notarized statement affirming just the opposite, and the Spiritualists made the most of this embarrassing piece of evidence.

With all the controversy, and with many, many guesses, some ingenious, as to how Ford got hold of the message, "Rosabelle believe," nobody was ever really able to pin down the truth. In spite of all the speculation and theories, until now the unanswered question remains: How did Arthur Ford get that message, which was supposed to be known only to the two Houdinis?

Now I am in a position to offer new evidence, which points to a reasonable and highly likely explanation.

In 1973, after the publication of Arthur Ford's biography,

I received a letter from a man named Jay Abbott, living in New York, who said he could shed some interesting light on the Houdini affair.

Mr. Abbott, since deceased, turned out to be an elderly but charming bachelor whose small apartment was festooned with pictures and other mementos of Arthur Ford and Beatrice Houdini. He had dozens of letters written to him by both people, Mrs. Houdini and Ford. These were couched in "Dear Jay" terms and showed a close and familiar relationship.

Jay Abbott, who, by the way, was a believing Spiritualist, told me some startling things about Arthur Ford and Beatrice Houdini. They were close friends, he said; in fact, "she was in love with Ford." He told me that they frequently dated before the famous séance, though usually with Ford using an alias.

Jay Abbott said that the night before the séance at which Arthur brought through the code message, he (Ford) and Beatrice were out dancing and both stumbled, and she hurt herself. This, said Abbott, was the "fall" that Mrs. Houdini suffered that was mentioned in the newspaper accounts of the séance.

How, then, did Ford get the secret words "Rosabelle believe" out of Mrs. Houdini? Did she conspire with him to dupe the public?

Jay Abbott, said he didn't believe that. Beatrice Houdini, he felt, had been duped by Arthur and only later realized it. Here is Abbott's version of how Ford got the key words:

"Beatrice told me that one day at her place she was washing her hands when her wedding ring slipped off her finger and fell to the floor. Ford, who was there, stooped down and picked it up.

"Engraved inside that ring, Beatrice said, was the key to the secret message. Probably that was when Ford got it. All he had to do was excuse himself for a moment—to get a towel, perhaps—and glance at the words inside the ring. Anyway, that is the way Mrs. Houdini herself told it to me.

"I believe I am the only one on earth who knows this directly from her own lips."

The "key" to the secret message inscribed in Bess Houdini's ring was the verse of a song:

> Rosabelle, sweet Rosabelle,
> I love you more than I can tell.
> Over me you cast a spell.
> I love you, my sweet Rosabelle.

This was supposed to be the first song that Houdini had heard his wife sing during their first show together years before. From this clue it was fairly simple, presumably, for Arthur Ford to deduce the rest of the secret message—the word "believe."

In Jay Abbott's version of the events, Mrs. Houdini initially seemed to accept the message through Ford as genuine, then came to doubt it, and finally to reject all alleged communications from her husband as spurious.

However, other knowledgeable people are less certain of Mrs. Houdini's innocence and sincerity. Close associates of Houdini, including the mentalist Dunninger and the scholarly and internationally famous author Walter B. Gibson (ghostwriter for Houdini, Thurston, Blackstone, and other noted magicians), have told me personally that they knew of Bess's close friendship with Arthur Ford. Their contention is that Mrs. Houdini, probably in the expectation that Ford would marry her, supplied him with the secret message. She was in collusion with him, in other words, to hoax the public.

Many magicians are said to have known of Bess Houdini's romantic involvement with Ford, yet none has seen fit to publicly reveal this fact, which is crucial for clearing up the mystery of how Ford got the secret message. Presumably these magicians were motivated by a desire to protect Bess Houdini's reputation—why, we shall probably never know. (Or was it, perhaps, a desire to protect the reputation of magic?)

What are we to say about this new evidence? How much credence can be put in Jay Abbot's story? Does it adequately explain the Houdini message?

Obviously, so long after the events, nobody who was not there can possibly say for sure what did or did not happen, but historians deal in probabilities and so must we.

Jay Abbott's story is plausible. His claim to have been on intimate terms with both Arthur Ford and Mrs. Houdini is beyond question, and his version of the strange episode certainly clears up the puzzle of how Ford got the secret words.

However, the theory that Mrs. Houdini was party to a conspiracy with Ford also explains this little matter. Which hypothesis the reader prefers—that Bess Houdini was duped by Ford or that she was in cahoots with him—is a matter of individual judgment based on all the evidence in the case, including these new revelations about the intimacy between Ford and Mrs. Houdini.

My personal view is that Mrs. Houdini entered into a plot with Arthur Ford to achieve fame and fortune by faking the ballyhooed, long-awaited message from her dead husband. No doubt Jay Abbott was sincere in his belief that Bess Houdini had been duped by Ford.

Knowing Arthur as I did for so long, I was aware that he was uncommonly touchy on the subject of the Houdini affair, as though he had a bad conscience about it. Certainly something made him wince every time it was brought up in conversation. From what we know now of his lamentable habit of cheating, he no doubt had cause to wince.

Am I dismayed that the evidence forces me to the conclusion that Arthur Ford faked the Houdini message?

No, I am sad but not dismayed. The truth can only make us stronger. The truth about Arthur Ford and mediumship in general is that where there is an unusual gift, there is also an unusual responsibility, and sometimes, alas, humanity is weak.

Especially mediums, of whom someone said: "Their weaknesses are very strong."

APPENDIX II
Books for Further Study

GENERAL TOPICS

Archer, Fred. *Exploring the Psychic World.* New York: William Morrow & Company, 1966.

——. *Crime and the Psychic World.* New York: William Morrow & Company, 1969.

Bach, Marcus. *The Power of Perception.* Garden City, N.Y.: Doubleday & Company, 1965.

Cayce, Hugh Lynn. *Venture Inward.* New York: Harper & Row, 1964.

De Lubac, Henri. *Teilhard de Chardin: The Man and His Meaning.* New York: Mentor, 1965 (paperback).

Durkin, Joseph T. *Hope for Our Time; Alexis Carrel on Man and Society.* New York: Harper & Row, 1965.

Ebon, Martin. *Prophecy in Our Time.* New York: New American Library, 1968.

——. *The Psychic Reader.* New York: World Publishing Company, 1969.

——. *They Knew the Unknown.* New York: World Publishing Company, 1971.

—— (ed). *The Psychic Scene.* New York: Signet (paperback), 1974.

Fodor, Nandor. *The Haunted Mind.* New York: Helix Press, 1959.

——. Encyclopaedia of Psychic Science. New Hyde Park, N.Y.: University Books, 1966.

——. *Freud, Jung, and Occultism.* New Hyde Park, N.Y.: University Books, 1971.

Garrett, Eileen J. *Beyond the Five Senses.* Philadelphia: J. B. Lippincott Company, 1957.

Gibson, Walter B. and Litzka, R. *The Complete Illustrated Book of the Psychic Sciences*. Garden City, N.Y.: Doubleday & Company, 1966.

Godwin, John. *Occult America*. Garden City, N.Y.: Doubleday & Company, 1972.

Higgins, Paul L. *Encountering the Unseen*. Minneapolis, Minn.: T. S. Denison & Company, 1966.

Holms, Campbell A. *The Facts of Psychic Science*. New Hyde Park, N.Y.: University Books, 1969.

Hudson, Thomas Jay. *The Law of Psychic Phenomena*. New York: Samuel Weiser, 1968.

Jung, C. G. *Memories, Dreams, Reflections*. New York: Pantheon Books, 1963.

Karagulla, Shafica. *Breakthrough to Creativity*. Los Angeles Calif.: DeVorss & Company, 1967.

Knight, David C. *The ESP Reader*. New York: Grosset & Dunlap, 1969.

McConnell, R. A. *ESP Curriculum Guide*. New York: Simon & Schuster, 1970.

Ornstein, Robert E. *The Nature of Human Consciousness*. San Francisco, Calif.: W. H. Freeman and Co., 1973 (paperback).

Ostrander, Sheila and Schroeder, Lynn. *Handbook of PSI Discoveries*. New York: G. P. Putnam's Sons, 1974.

Parente, Pascal P. *Beyond Space, A Book About the Angels*. Rockford, Illinois: Tan Books and Publishers, Inc. 1973.

Ramsey, Arthur Michael. *The Glory of God and the Transfiguration of Christ*. London: Longmans, Green & Company, 1949.

Schwarz, Berthold. *Parent-Child Telepathy*. New York: Garrett Publications, 1971.

Sherman, Harold. *Your Mysterious Powers of ESP*. New York: World Publishing Company, 1969.

Smith, Alson J. *Religion and the New Psychology*. Garden City, N.Y.: Doubleday & Company, 1951.

Smith, Susy. *ESP*. New York: Pyramid Publications, 1962 (paperback).

Spraggett, Allen. *The Unexplained*. New York: New American Library, 1967.

——. *The Bishop Pike Story*. New York: Signet, 1970 (paperback).

Tompkins, Peter. *The Secret Life of Plants*. New York: Harper & Row, 1974.

Vaughan, Alan. *Patterns of Prophecy*. New York: Hawthorn Books, 1974.

Watson, Lyall, *Super Nature*. New York: Anchor Press /Doubleday, 1973.

Woods, Richard. *The Occult Revolution*. New York: Herder and Herder, 1971.

Worrall, Ambrose and Olga with Oursler, Will. *Explore Your Psychic World*. New York: Harper & Row, 1970.

PRAYER, MYSTICISM, MEDITATION, AND THE SPIRITUAL LIFE

Bach, Marcus. *The Inner Ecstasy*. New York: World Publishing Company, 1969.

Bro, Harmon. *Dreams in the Life of Prayer*. New York: Harper & Row, 1970.

Bucke, Richard Maurice. *Cosmic Consciousness*. New York: E. P. Dutton & Company, 1901.

Crookall, Robert. *Interpretation of Cosmic and Mystical Experience*. London: James Clarke, 1969.

Fremantle, Anne. *The Protestant Mystics*. Boston: Little, Brown and Company 1964.

Garrett, Eileen J. *Awareness*. New York: Helix Press, 1943.

Goldsmith, Joel S. *The Art of Meditation*. New York: Harper & Brothers, 1956.

Guardini, Romano. *Prayer in Practice*. New York: Pantheon Books, 1957.

Hall, Manly P. *The Mystical Christ*. California: The Philosophical Research Society, 1956.

Hamman, A. *Prayer the New Testament*. Chicago: Franciscan Herald Press, 1971.

Happold, F. C. *Mysticism*. London: Penguin Books, 1964 (paperback).

Inge, W. R. *Christian Mysticism*. New York: Meridian Books, 1956.

———. *Mysticism in Religion*. London: Rider & Company, 1969 (paperback).

Israel, Martin *An Approach to Mysticism*. London: Churches Fellowship, 1968.

———. *An Approach to Spirituality*. London: Churches Fellowship, 1971.

Israel, Martin. *Summons to Life*. The Search for Identity through the Spiritual. London: Hodder and Stoughton, 1974.

James, William. *The Varieties of Religious Experience*. New Hyde Park, N.Y.: University Books, 1963.

Johnson, Raynor C. *The Imprisoned Splendour*. New York: Harper & Brothers, 1953.

———. *Watcher on the Hills*. New York: Harper & Brothers, 1959.

Jones, Rufus. *Studies in Mystical Religion*. London: Macmillan & Company, 1923.

Kimmell, Jo. *Steps to Prayer Power*. Nashville-Abingdon Press, 1972 (paperback).

Loehr, Franklin. *The Power of Prayer on Plants*. New York: Signet 1959 (paperback).

Masters, Robert and Houston, Jean. *Mind Games*. New York: The Viking Press, 1972.

Parker, William R. and St. Johns, Elaine. *Prayer Can Change Your Life*. Englewood Cliffs, N.J.: Prentice-Hall, 1957.

Powers, Thomas E. *First Questions on the Life of the Spirit*. New York: Harper & Brothers, 1959.

Shoemaker, Samuel M. *With the Holy Spirit and with Fire*. New York: Harper & Brothers, 1960.

Stace, Walter T. *The Teachings of the Mystics*. New York: Mentor Books, 1960.

Strong, Mary, ed. *Letters of the Scattered Brotherhood*, New York: Harper & Brothers, 1948.

Thurston, Herbert. *The Physical Phenomena of Mysticism*. Chicago: Henry Regnery Company, 1952.

Underhill, Evelyn. *Worship*. New York: Harper & Brothers, 1937.

———. *Practical Mysticism*. New York: E. P. Dutton & Company, 1943 (paperback).

———. *Mysticism.* New York: The Noonday Press, 1955 (paper-backs).

———. *The Mystics of the Church.* New York: Schocken Books, 1964 (paperback).

White, John, ed. *What Is Meditation?* Garden City, N.Y. Anchor Press/Doubleday & Company, (paperback).

FAMOUS PSYCHICS, THEIR LIFE AND WORK

Angoff, Allan. *Eileen Garrett and the World Beyond the Senses.* New York: William Morrow & Company, 1974.

Bird, J. Malcolm. *Margery the Medium.* Boston: Small, Maynard & Company, 1925.

Brown, Rosemary. *Unfinished Symphonies.* London: Souvenir Press, 1971.

Cummins, Geraldine. *Unseen Adventures.* London: Rider & Company, 1951.

Feilding, Everard. *Sitting with Eusapia Palladino.* New Hyde Park, N.Y.: University Books, 1963.

Ford, Arthur with Bro, Margueritte. *Nothing so Strange.* New York: Harper & Brothers, 1958.

Garrett, Eileen J. *My Life as a Search for the Meaning of Mediumship.* London: Rider & Company, 1939.

———. *Many Voices: The Autobiography of a Medium.* New York: G. P. Putnam's Sons, 1968.

Home, Daniel D. *Incidents in My Life.* Secaucus, N.J.: University Books.

Leonard, Gladys Osborne. *My Life in Two Worlds.* London: Cassell & Company, 1931.

Montgomery, Ruth. *A Gift of Prophecy.* New York: William Morrow & Company, 1965.

Progoff, Ira. *The Image of an Oracle: A Report on Research into the Mediumship of Eileen J. Garrett.* New York: Helix Press, 1964.

Psychic Magazine, eds. *Psychics.* In Depth Interviews. New York: Harper & Row, 1972.

Smith, Eleanor Touhey. *Psychic People.* New York: William Morrow & Company, 1968.

Smith, Susy, *The Mediumship of Mrs. Leonard*. New Hyde
  Park, N.Y.: University Books, 1964.

Spraggett, Allen with Rauscher, William V. *Arthur Ford: The
  Man Who Talked with The Dead*. New York: New American Library, 1973.

Sugrue, Thomas. *There is a River*. New York: Holt, Rinehart
  & Winston, 1942.

Tietze, Thomas R. *Margery*. New York: Harper & Row, 1973.

Twigg, Ena with Brod, Ruth Hagy. *Ena Twigg: Medium*.
  New York: Hawthorn Books, 1972.

ASTRAL PROJECTION

Crookall, Robert. *A Study and Practice of Astral Projection*.
  London: The Aquarian Press, 1960.

———. *The Techniques of Astral Projection*. London: The
  Aquarian Press, 1964.

———. *More Astral Projections*. London: The Aquarian Press,
  1964.

———. *During Sleep*. London: Theosophical Publishing House,
  1964 (paperback).

———. *The Mechanisms of Astral Projection*. Moradabad, In-
  dia: Darshana, 1968.

Hart, Hornell. "ESP Projection—Spontaneous Cases and Re-
  peatable Experiments." New York: American Society for
  Psychical Research, 1953 (mimeograph report).

Monroe, Robert A. *Journeys out of the Body*. Garden City
  N.Y.: Anchor Press/Doubleday & Company, 1973 (paperback).

Muldoon, Sylvan J. and Carrington, Hereward. *The Projection of the Astral Body*. London: Rider & Company, 1929.

Smith, Susy. *The Enigma of out-of-Body Travel*. New York:
  Helix Press, 1965.

LIFE AFTER DEATH

Bayless, Raymond. *The Other Side of Death*. New Hyde
  Park, N.Y.: University Books, 1971.

Beard, Paul. *Survival of Death*. London: Hodder and Stoughton, 1966.

Ducasse, C. J. *A Critical Examination of the Belief in a Life After Death*. Springfield, Illinois: Charles C. Thomas, Publisher, 1961.

Eddy, Sherwood. *You Will Survive After Death*. New York: Rinehart & Company, 1950.

Ford, Arthur as told to Ellison, Jerome. *The Life Beyond Death*. New York: G. P. Putnam's Sons, 1971.

Garrett, Eileen, J., ed. *Does Man Survive Death?* New York: Helix Press, 1957.

Harlow, S. Ralph. *A Life After Death*. Garden City, N.Y.: Doubleday & Company, 1961.

Hart, Hornell. *The Enigma of Survival—the Case for and Against an After Life*. Springfield, Ill. Charles C Thomas, 1959.

Matthews, W. R. *The Hope of Immortality*. New York: Morehouse Barlow Company, 1966.

Mundy, Jon. *Learning to Die*. Evanston, Ill. Spiritual Frontiers Fellowship, Inc., 1973.

Myers, F. W. H. *Human Personality and Its Survival of Bodily Death*. ed. Susy Smith. New Hyde Park, N.Y.: University Books, 1961.

Pike, James A. *The Other Side*. Garden City, N.Y.: Doubleday & Company, 1969.

Ramsey, Arthur Michael. *The Resurrection of Christ*. London: Fontana Books, 1961 (paperback).

Smith, Alson J. *Immortality: The Scientific Evidence*. New York: Prentice-Hall, Inc. 1954.

Smyth, J. Paterson. *The Gospel of the Hereafter*. London: Hodder and Stoughton, no date.

Spraggett, Allen. *The Case for Immortality*. New York: New American Library, 1974.

Weatherhead, Leslie D. *The Christian Agnostic*. London: Hodder and Stoughton, 1965.

SPIRITUALISM

Barbanell, Maurice. *This Is Spiritualism*. London: Herbert Jenkins, 1959.

Brown, Slater. *The Heyday of Spiritualism.* New York: Hawthorn Books, 1970.

Carrington, Hereward. *The Physical Phenomena of Spiritualism.* New York: American Universities Publishing Co., 1920.

Dunninger, Joseph. *Inside the Medium's Cabinet.* New York: David Kemp & Company, 1935.

Edmunds, Simeon. *Spiritualism: A Critical Survey.* London: The Aquarian Press, 1966.

Jackson, Herbert G. *The Spirit Rappers.* Garden City, N.Y.: Doubleday & Company, 1972.

Kerr, Howard. *Mediums and Spirit-Rappers, and Roaring Radicals.* Chicago: University of Illinois Press, 1972.

Knight, Marcus. *Spiritualism Reincarnation and Immortality.* London: Gerald Duckworth & Company, Ltd., 1950.

Longridge, George. *Spiritualism and Christianity.* London: A. R. Mowbray & Company Ltd., 1926.

McHargue, Georgess. *Facts, Frauds, and Phantasms: A Survey of the Spiritualist Movement.* Garden City, N.Y.: Doubleday & Company, 1972.

Proskauer, Julien J. *Spook Crooks!* New York: A. L. Burt Company, 1932.

Somerlott, Robert. *"Here, Mr. Splitfoot."* New York: The Viking Press, 1971.

Spraggett, Allen and Rauscher, William V. *The Psychic Mafia.* New York: Harper & Row, 1975.

Thurston, Herbert. *The Church and Spiritualism.* Milwaukee, Wis.: Bruce Publishing Company, 1933.

REINCARNATION

Beddoes, Thomas P. *Reincarnation and Christian Tradition, An Annotated Bibliography.* Washington D.C.: The Department of Library Science of the Catholic University of America. Research Paper, 1970.

Cerminara, Gina. *Many Mansions.* New York: William Sloane Associates, 1950.

Dixon, Jeane. *Reincarnation and Prayers to Live By.* New York: William Morrow & Company, 1970.

Ebon, Martin. ed. *Reincarnation in the Twentieth Century.* New York: World Publishing Company, 1969.

Head, Joseph and Cranston, S. L., ed. and comps. *Reincarnation: An East-West Anthology.* New York: The Julian Press, 1961.

Knight, Marcus. *Spiritualism, Reincarnation and Immortality.* London: Gerald Duckworth & Company, 1950.

Martin, Eva, ed. *Reincarnation—the Ring of Return.* New Hyde Park, N.Y.: University Books, 1963.

Stevenson, Ian. *Twenty Cases Suggestive of Reincarnation.* New York: American Society for Psychical Research, 1966.

Two Articles on Reincarnation—"Reincarnation: Fact or Fantasy" by Hereward Carrington and "The Western Way with Reincarnation" by J. Gordon Melton. Booklet. Memphis, Tenn.: J. Gordon Melton, Publisher, 1971.

Weatherhead, Leslie D. *The Case for Reincarnation.* Surrey, England: M. C. Petro, 1958.

THE PSYCHIC, THE BIBLE, AND RELIGION

Bazak, Jacob. *Judaism and Psychical Phenomena.* New York: Garrett Publications. 1972.

Carrington, Hereward. *Loaves and Fishes.* New York: Charles Scribner's Sons, 1935.

Cummins, Geraldine. *The Scripts of Cleophas.* London: Psychic Press Ltd., 1961.

Elliott, Maurice. *The Bible as Psychic History.* London: Rider & Company, 1959.

———. *The Psychic Life of Jesus.* London: Spiritualist Press, 1938.

Heron, Laurence Tunstall. *ESP in the Bible: The Psychic Roots of Religion.* Garden City, N.Y.: Doubleday & Company, 1974.

Higgins, Paul L. *Mother of All.* Minneapolis, Minn.: T. S. Denison & Company, Inc., 1969.

Macdonald, J. *Psychical Experience and Christian Investiga-*

tion. London. The Churches Fellowship, 1962 (pamphlet).

Malcolm, James F. *Christianity and Psychic Facts.* Manchester, England: The Spiritualists National Union. no date (paperback).

Neff, Richard H. *Psychic Phenomena and Religion.* Philadelphia: The Westminster Press, 1971.

Pearce-Higgins, J. D., ed. *Life, Death and Psychical Research.* London: Rider & Company, 1973 (paperback).

Rhine, J. B. "Can Parapsychology Help Religion?" *Spiritual Frontiers,* Winter 1974.

Stobart, St. Clair. *Ancient Lights.* New York: E. P. Dutton & Company, 1923

Weatherhead, Leslie E. *The Manner of the Resurrection.* New York: Abingdon Press, 1959.

MAGIC AND MENTALISM

(Includes Methods Used by Entertainers and Fraudulent Mediums)

Annemann, Theodore. *Practical Mental Effects.* New York: Holden's Magic Shops, 1944.

Cannell, J. C. *The Secrets of Houdini.* New York: Dover Publications, 1973.

Christopher, Milbourne. *Houdini: The Untold Story.* New York: Thomas Y. Crowell Company, 1969.

———. *Esp, Seers & Psychics.* New York: Thomas Y. Crowell Company, 1970.

———. *The Illustrated History of Magic.* New York: Thomas Y. Crowell Company, 1973.

Corinda. *Thirteen Steps to Mentalism.* New York: Louis Tannen, 1968.

Curry, P. *Magician's Magic.* New York: Franklin Watts. 1965.

Dunninger, to Gibson, Walter. *Dunninger's Secrets.* Secaucus, N.J.: Lyle Stuart, 1974.

Gibson, Walter. *The Master Magicians.* Garden City, N.Y.: Doubleday & Company, 1966.

Gibson, Walter & Young, Morris. *Houdini on Magic.* New York: Dover Publications, 1953.

Gresham, William Lindsay. *Houdini: The Man Who Walked Through Walls.* New York: Hillman Books, 1961 (paperback).

Houdini, Harry. *A Magician Among the Spirits.* New York: Arno Press, 1972.

Hull, Burling. *Encyclopedic Dictionary of Mentalism,* Vols. 1 and 2. Canada: Calgary, Alberta, Canada: Micky Hades Enterprises, 1972–73.

Kellock, Harold. *Houdini.* New York: Harcourt, Brace & Company, 1928.

Kreskin. *The Amazing World of Kreskin.* New York: Random House, 1973.

POSSESSION AND EXORCISM

Ebon, Martin. *The Devil's Bride.* (*Exorcism: Past and Present*). New York: Harper & Row, 1974.

———. *Exorcism: Fact not Fiction.* New York: Signet Books, 1974 (paperback).

Fortune, Dion. *Psychic Self-Defense.* London: The Aquarian Press, 1963.

Koch, Kurt E. *Christian Counseling and Occultism.* Grand Rapids: Kregel Publication, 1965.

Neil-Smith, Christopher. *The Exorcist and the Possessed.* St. Ives, Cornwall, England: James Pike Ltd., 1974.

Nicola, John J. *Diabolical Possession and Exorcism.* Rockford, Ill.: Tan Books, 1974 (paperback).

Oesterreich, T. K. *Obsession and Possession by Spirits Both Good and Evil.* Chicago: The de Laurence Company, 1935.

Pearce-Higgins, John D. "Twentieth-Century Exorcism" *Spiritual Frontiers,* Winter 1969.

Petitpierre, Dom Robert, ed. *Exorcism: The Findings of a Commission* (convened by the bishop of Exeter). London: S.P.C.K., 1972 (paperback).

Richards, John. *But Deliver Us from Evil, An introduction to the demonic dimension in pastoral care.* London: Darton Longman & Todd, 1974.

Wickland, Carl A. *Thirty Years Among the Dead*. London: Spiritualist Press, 1968.

Woods, Richard. *The Devil*. Chicago: The Thomas More Press, 1973.

HYPNOTISM

Arons, Harry, and Bubeck, M. F. H. *Handbook of Professional Hypnosis*. Irvington, N.J.: Power Publishers, Inc., 1971.

Bernheim, H. *Hypnosis & Suggestion in Psychotheraphy, a Treatise on the Nature and Uses of Hypnotism*. New Hyde Park, N.Y.: University Books, 1964.

Berstein, Morey. *The Search for Bridey Murphy*. Garden City, N.Y.: Doubleday & Company, Inc., 1956.

Cannon, Alexander. *The Science of Hypnotism*. New York: E. P. Dutton & Company, Inc., 1946.

Cuddon, Eric. *Hypnosis, Its Meaning and Practice*. London: G. Bell & Sons, Ltd., 1957.

Edmunds, Simeon. *Hypnosis: Key to Psychic Powers*. London: The Aquarian Press, 1968 (paperback).

Gibson, Walter B. *Hypnotism*. New York: Grosset & Dunlap, Inc., 1970.

Hypnotism. A Psychic Malpractice. Los Angeles, Calif.: The Theosophy Company (no date, no author, booklet).

Jensen, Ann, and Watkins, Mary Lou. *Franz Anton Mesmer, Physician Extraordinaire*. New York: Garrett Publications /Helix Press, 1967.

Podmore, Frank. *From Mesmer to Christian Science, A Short History of Mental Healing*. New Hyde Park, N.Y.: University Books, 1963.

Wittkofski, Joseph. *The Pastoral Use of Hypnotic Technique*. New York: The MacMillan Company, 1961.

GHOSTS AND POLTERGEISTS

Bardens, Dennis. *Ghosts and Hauntings*. New York: Taplinger Publishing Company, 1968.

Fodor, Nandor. *On the Trail of the Poltergeist*. New York: Citadel Press, 1958.

Norman, Diana. *The Stately Ghosts of England*. London: Frederik Muller Ltd., 1963.

Owen, A. R. G. *Can We Explain the Poltergeist?* New York: Helix Press, 1964.

Owen, A. R. G. and Sims, Victor. *Science and the Spook*. New York: Garrett Publications, 1972.

Price, Harry. *The Most Haunted House in England*. London: Longmans, Green Company, 1941.

Roll, William G. *The Poltergeist*. New York: Signet 1972 (paperback).

Stevens, William O. *Unbidden Guests*. New York: Dodd, Mead & Company, 1945.

Thurston, Herbert. *Ghosts and Poltergeists*. London: Burns Oates, 1955.

Tyrrell, G. N. M. *Apparitions*. London: Gerald Duckworth & Company Ltd., 1943.

HEALING

Academy of Parapsychology and Medicine. *The Dimensions of Healing*. Calif.: privately published, 1972 (paperback).

———. *The Varieties of Healing Experience*. Los Altos, Calif.: privately published, 1971 (paperback).

Arnold, Dorothy Musgrave. *Called by Christ to Heal*. New York: The Seabury Press, 1965.

Edwards, Harry. *The Power of Spiritual Healing*. London: Herbert Jenkins, 1963.

Gross, Don H. *The Case for Spiritual Healing*. New York: Thomas Nelson & Sons, 1958.

Garrett, Eileen J. *Life Is the Healer*. Philadelphia: Dorrance & Company, 1957.

Hall, Manly P. *Healing: The Divine Art*. Los Angeles: Philosophical Research Society, 1950.

Hammond, Sally. *We Are All Healers*. New York: Harper & Row, 1973.

Ikin, A. Graham. *Studies in Spiritual Healing*. London: The World Fellowship Press for The Churches Fellowship, 1968 (paperback).

Israel, Martin. *Healing and the Spirit*. London: Churches Fellowship for Pyschical and Spiritual Studies, 1972, Booklet.

Melton, J. Gordon. *A Reader's Guide to the Church's Ministry of Healing*. Evanston, Ill.: The Academy of Religion and Psychical Research., 1973.

Neal, Emily Gardiner. *The Healing Power of Christ*. New York: Hawthorn Books, 1972.

Sanford, Agnes. *The Healing Power of the Bible*. Philadelphia: J. B. Lippincott Company, 1969.

Sanford, Edgar L. *God's Healing Power*. Englewood Cliffs, N.J.: Prentice-Hall, 1959.

Sherman, Harold. *Your Power to Heal*. New York: Harper & Row, 1972.

Spraggett, Allen. *Kathryn Kuhlman: The Woman Who Believes in Miracles*. New York: World Publishing Company, 1970.

Turner, Gordon. *An Outline of Spiritual Healing*. London: Psychic Press, 1970.

Worrall, Ambrose and Olga. *The Gift of Healing*. New York: Harper & Row, 1965.

Weatherhead, Leslie D. *Psychology, Religion, and Healing*. Nashville, Tenn.: Abingdon Press, 1962 (paperback).

West, Donald J. *Eleven Lourdes Miracles*. New York: Helix Press, 1957.

PSYCHIC RESEARCH AND PARAPSYCHOLOGY

Ashby, Robert H. *The Guide Book for the Study of Psychical Research*. New York: Samuel Weiser, 1972.

Bayless, Raymond. *Experiences of a Psychical Researcher*. New Hyde Park, New York: University Books, Inc. 1972.

Broad, C. D. *Lectures on Psychical Research*. London: Routledge & Kegan Paul, 1962.

Gauld, Alan. *The Founders of Psychical Research*. London: Routledge & Kegan Paul, 1968.

Greenhouse, Herbert B. *The Book of Psychic Knowledge, All Your Questions Answered*. New York: Taplinger Publishing Company, 1973.

Hankey, Muriel. *J. Hewat McKenzie, Pioneer of Psychical Research*. London: The Aquarian Press, 1963.

Johnson, R. C. *Psychical Research*. London: The English Universities Press Ltd., 1964.

LeShan, Lawrence. *The Medium, the Mystic, and the Physicist: Toward A General Theory of the Paranormal*. New York: The Viking Press, 1974.

Muhl, Anita M. *Automatic Writing*. New York: Helix Press, 1953, 1963.

Murphy, Gardner and Ballou, Robert O., eds. *William James on Psychical Research*. New York: The Viking Press, 1960.

————. *Challenge of Psychical Research*. New York: Harper & Brothers, 1961.

Mitchell, Edgar D. et al. with White, John, eds. *Psychic Exploration*. New York: G. P. Putnam's Sons, 1974.

Osis, Karlis. *Deathbed Observations by Physicians and Nurses*. New York: Parapsychology Foundation, 1961 (paperback).

Ostrander, Sheila and Schroeder, Lynn. *Psychic Discoveries Behind the Iron Curtain*. Englewood Cliffs, N.J. Prentice-Hall, 1970.

————. *Handbook of Psi Discoveries*. New York: G. P. Putnam's Sons, 1974.

Pratt, Gaither J. *Parapsychology: An Insider's View of ESP*. Garden City, N.Y.: Doubleday & Company, 1964.

Rhine, J. B. *New World of the Mind*. New York: William Sloane Associates, 1953 (paperback).

————. *The Reach of the Mind*. New York: William Sloane Associates, 1960.

————. *Extrasensory Preception*. Boston: Bruce Humphries, 1964.

Rhine, J. B. and Brier, Robert, eds. *Parapsychology Today*. New York: Citadel Press, 1968.

Rhine, Louisa E. *Mind over Matter*. New York: The Macmillan Company, 1970.

Schmeidler, Gertrude, ed. *Extrasensory Perception*. Chicago: Atherton Press, 1969.

Sudre, Rene, *Parapsychology*. New York: Citadel Press, 1960.

Tabori, Paul. *Pioneers of the Unseen.* New York: Taplinger Publishing Company, 1972.

Tenhaeff, W. H. C. *Telepathy and Clairvoyance.* Springfield, Ill.: Charles C Thomas, 1972.

Ullman, Montague and Krippner, Stanley with Vaughan, Alan. *Dream Telepathy.* New York: The Macmillan Company, 1973.

APPENDIX III

Organizations and Publications Devoted to Psychic Phenomena and Related Topics

Write to the following for more information about parapsychology, psychic phenomena, ESP, and related topics. (This list of psychically oriented organizations is not to be construed as implying any necessary endorsement of a particular organization by the author but is for the reader's convenience only.)

Academy of Parapsychology and Medicine Proceedings
314 Second Street
Los Altos, Calif. 94022

Academy of Religion and Psychical Research Proceedings
800 Custer Avenue
Evanston, Ill. 60202

American Society for Psychical Research Journal
5 West 73rd Street
New York, N.Y. 10023

Association for Research and Enlightenment Journal
The Edgar Cayce Foundation
Virginia Beach, Va. 23451

Churches' Fellowship for Psychical and Quarterly review
Spiritual Studies
St. Mary Abchurch
Abchurch Lane
London EC4N 7BA
England